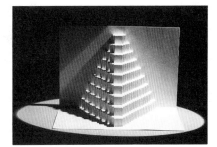

POP-up
GREETING CARDS

A CREATIVE PERSONAL TOUCH FOR EVERY OCCASION

ORIGAMIC ARCHITECTURE BY MASAHIRO CHATANI

CONTENTS

Message from the Author

Soon after "Origamic Architecture of Pop-up Cards" drew attention at the shop of the Museum of Modern Art in New York, the English and the Dutch editions of my book were published. Now I am pleased to present this new one as a sequel, complying with the request of many people. This is the seventh pop-up-card book I have designed, according to an article in Asahi, one of the biggest newspapers in Japan, pop-up cards are getting more and more popular. Thus the imaginative world created with Kent paper is becoming bigger and wider.

I have been so devoted to designing pop-up cards recently that I am at a loss when asked which is my regular job, building houses with iron and wood or making houses with paper. I had exhibitions of my cards in New York around Christmastime last year, at Harvard University this spring and now I am traveling around Copenhagen, The Hague, Geneva and Rome to show my works.

This sequel has sixty pieces, from standard modern architecture to improvised pieces, particularly such a work as "Three-dimensional form", shown on the cover and also in actual-size pattern, a unique feature of this book. I would like to give all of you the pleasure of folding everything in the world within the space of two post-cards. It is fun to see what appears when the card is opened, but you will find it even more enjoyable when you make the cards by yourself. In addition. I am sure everybody will feel great pleasure in sending his or her own cards to special friends.

September, 1986 Masahiro Chatani

Author: Masahiro Chatani
1967: Doctor of Engineering
1977: Visiting Associate Professor, University of Washington at Seattle
1980~: Professor, Tokyo Institute of Technology

★ Copyright © 1986 MASAHIRO CHATANI & ONDORISHA PUBLISHERS, LTD. All rights reserved.
★ Published by ONDORISHA PUBLISHERS, LTD., 32 Nishigoken-cho, Shinjuku-ku, Tokyo 162, Japan.
★ Sole Overseas Distributor: Japan Publications Trading Co., Ltd.
  P. O. Box 5030 Tokyo International, Tokyo, Japan.
★ Distributed in the United States by Kodansha International / USA, Ltd.
  through Harper & Row, Publishers, Inc., 10 East 53rd Street, New York, New York 10022.
  Australia by Bookwise International, 1 Jeanes Street, Beverley, South Australia 5007, Australia.

10 9 8 7 6 5 4 3 2

ISBN 0-87040-733-3
Printed in Japan

Automobile Pavilion

Instructions on pages 81-83.

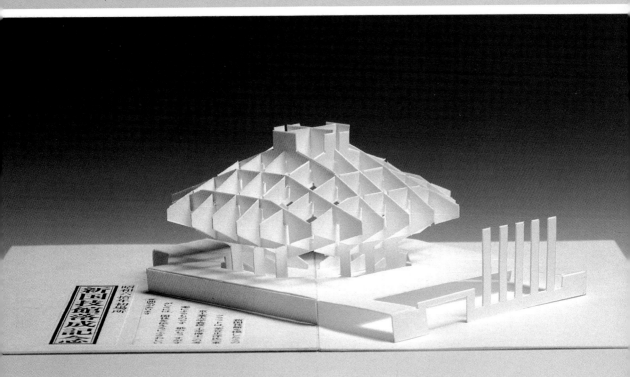

Sumo Stadium

Instructions on pages 84-87.

5

Big Ben

Instructions on page 33.

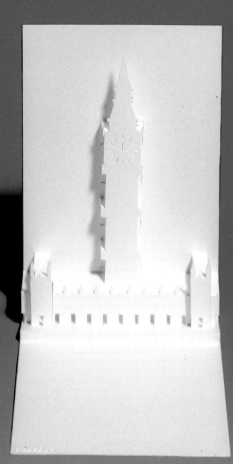

London Bridge

Instructions on page 26.

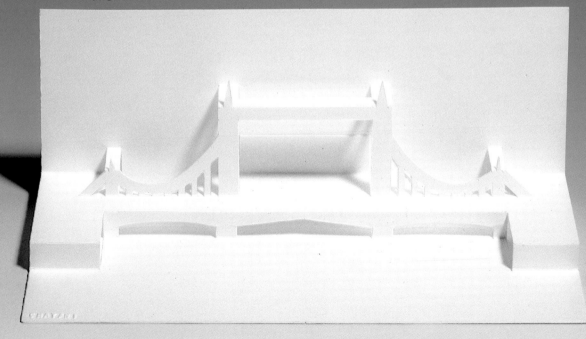

Globe

Instructions on pages 76-77.

3-D Fan

Unfolding process
of the above card

Instructions on pages 78-79.

7

Various Forms: Form A

Instructions on page 28.

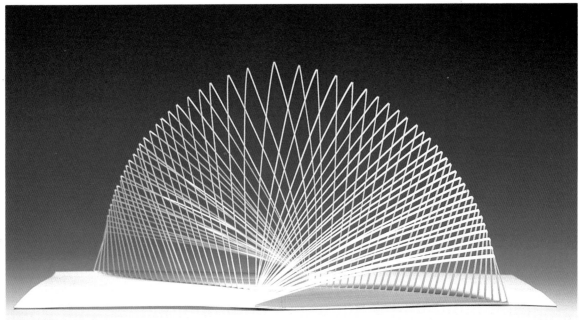

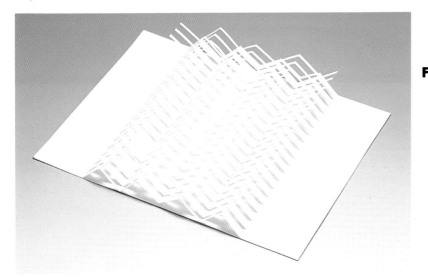

Form B

Instructions on page 70.

The photo shows when the above cards
A and B are opened to 90 degrees.

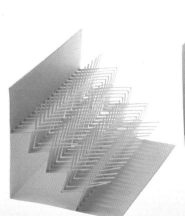

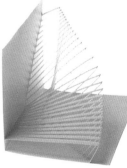

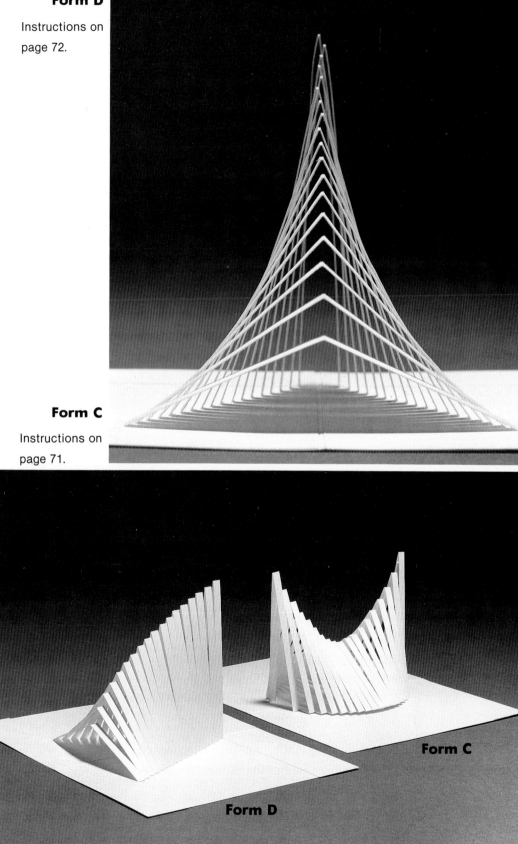

Form D

Instructions on page 72.

Form C

Instructions on page 71.

House on Stilts

Instructions on pages 74–75.

New Year's Pine Decoration

Instructions on page 30.

Slope A

Instructions on page 73.

Slope B

Instructions on page 80.

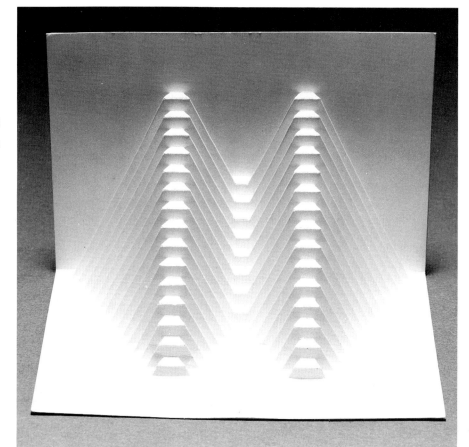

Twin Peaks

Instructions on page 34.

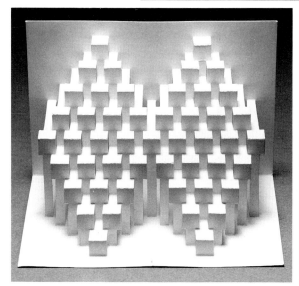

Montage A

Instructions on page 35.

Montage B

Instructions on page 89.

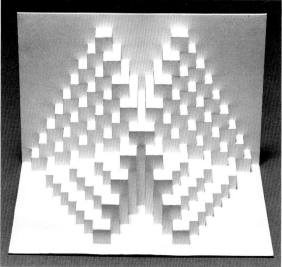

Jungle-gym

Instructions on page 36.

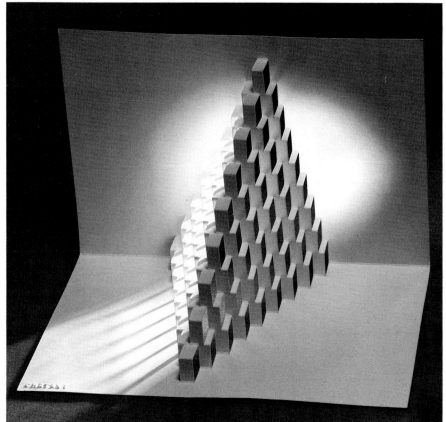

Tumbling Blocks

Instructions on page 37.

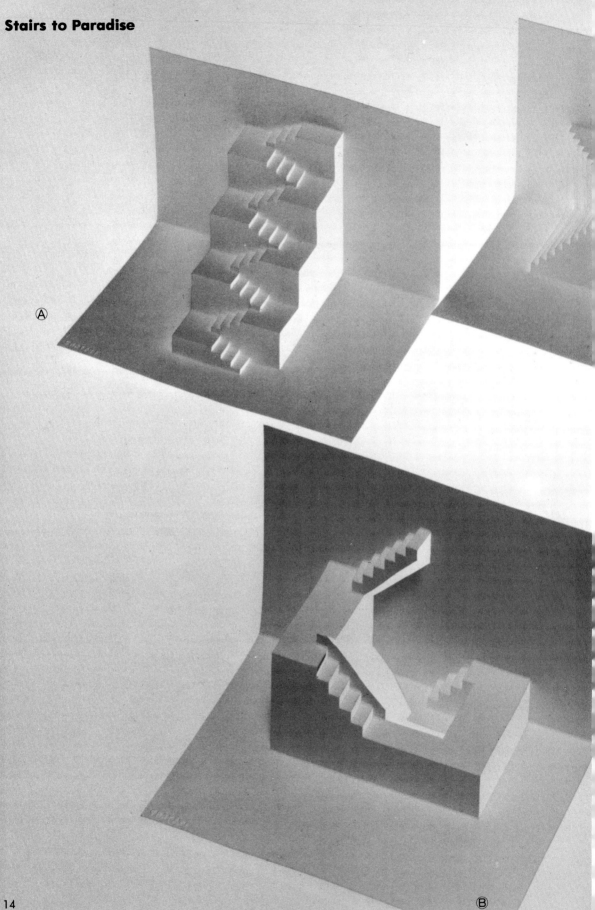

Instructions for A on page 38,
for B on page 39,
for C on page 40,
for D on page 90 and
for E on page 41.

Ⓒ

Ⓓ

Ⓔ

Chairs

Instructions on pages 42–43.

Beds

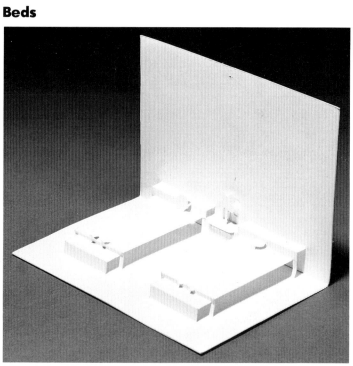

Instructions on page 45.

Dresser

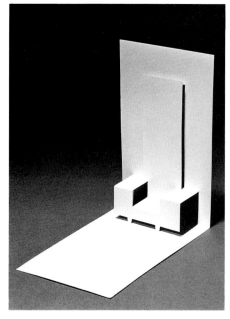

Instructions on page 44.

Children's Room

Instructions on page 46.

Dining Car

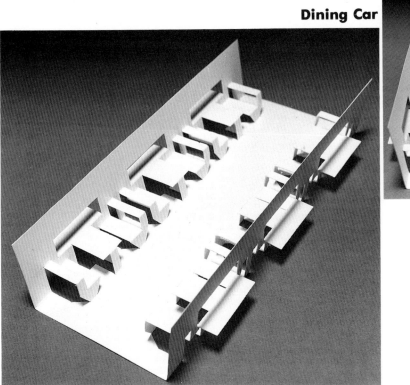

Instructions on page 91.

**Steam
Locomotive**

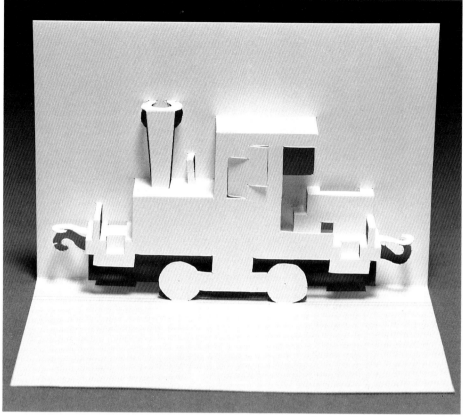

Instructions on page 47.

**Passenger
Car**

Instructions on page 48

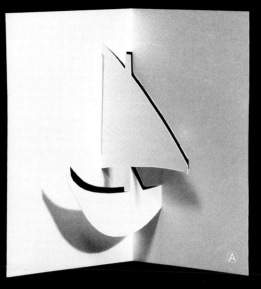

Instructions on page 49.

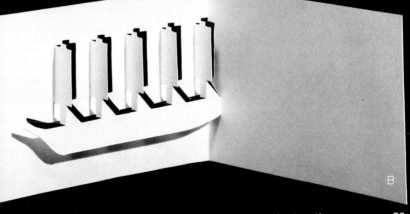

Instructions on page 50.

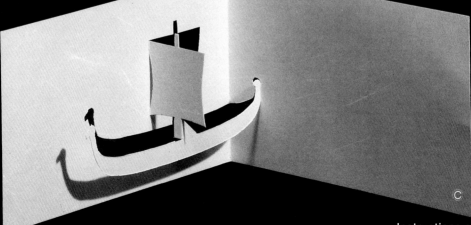

Instructions on page 51.

Circular Construction

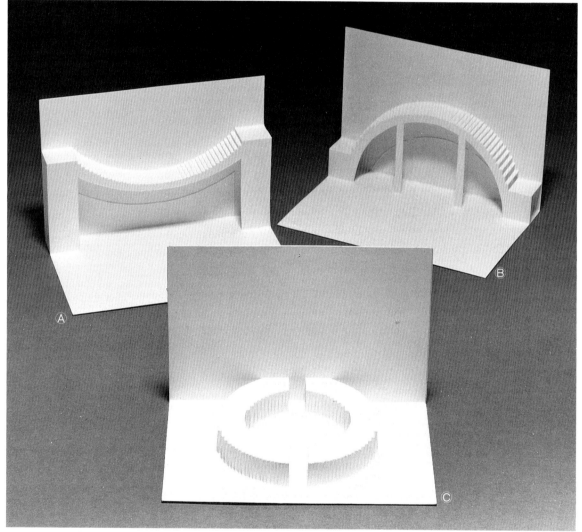

Instructions for A on page 52,
for B on page 92 and
for C on page 53.

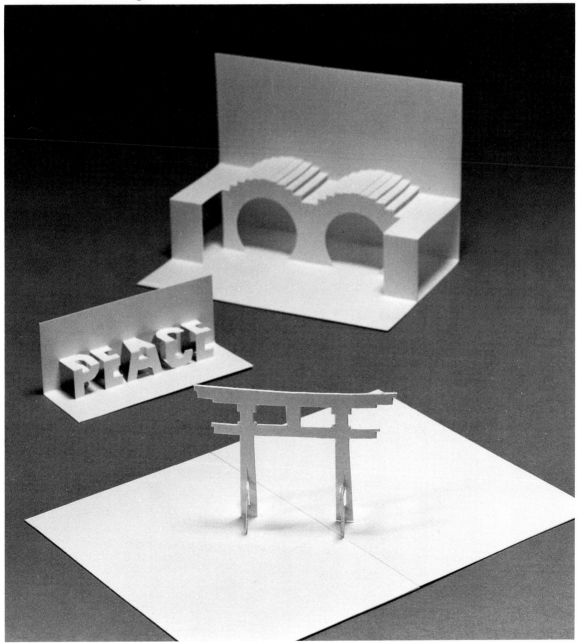

PEACE   **Shinto Shrine Archway**

Instructions on page 63.   Instructions on page 55.

Clever World

Ⓐ Cutlery Set　　　　**Ⓑ Comb**

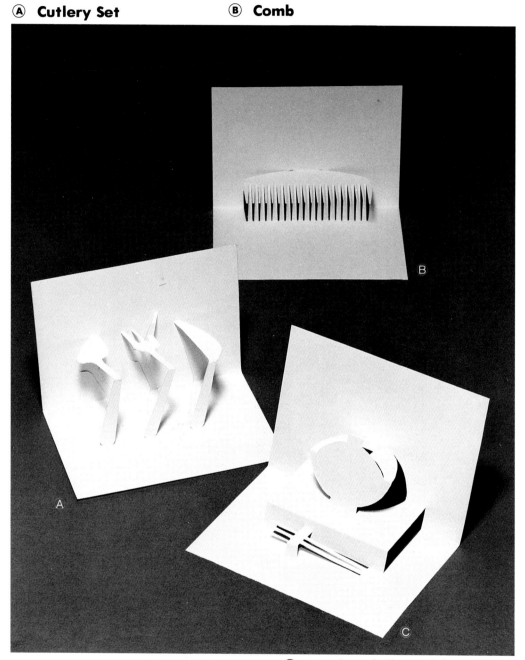

Ⓒ Bowl and Chopsticks

Instructions for A on page 56,
　　　　for B on page 57 and
　　　　for C on page 58.

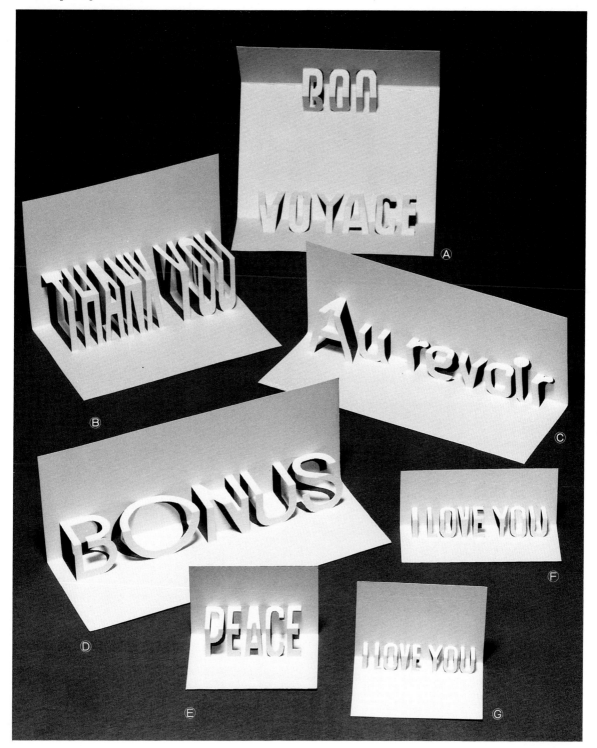

Instructions for A on page 59,
for B on page 60,
for C on page 61,
for D on page 62,
for E, F, and G on page 63.

Instructions for Ⓐ Gladiolus on page 64, for Ⓑ Lily of the Valley on page 65, for Ⓒ Rose on page 66, for Ⓓ Hibiscus on page 67, for Ⓔ Dahlia on page 68, and for Ⓕ Azalea on page 69.

Basics in Origamic Architecture

Materials and Tools:

All the works shown in this book can be made with simple materials and tools. Your hands and head are the most important tools. However, the following materials and tools are required for the best results.

To make the 90° open type card:

1. Kent paper (To make a sample, use drawing paper or graph paper.)
2. Sketch pad
3. Graph paper (1mm square)
4. Pencil (HB or H)
5. Eraser
6. Tracing paper
7. Clear plastic ruler
8. Steel ruler
9. Protractor
10. Cutting knife (Circle cutter works well for curves.)
11. Thick and thin stylus pen
12. Clear adhesive tape
13. Compasses
14. Pointed tweezers
15. All-purpose glue

To make the 180° open type card:

The following tool and materials are required in addition to those above.

1. Japanese rice paper
2. White cotton thread
3. Calculator

About the paper:

Most of the works in this book are made of medium-weight white Kent paper of double-postcard size (20cm by 15cm) (8″×16″). Very thick paper is not advisable for such pieces which need backing. For 90° open types, colored Kent paper or colored drawing paper can add an interesting effect when used for backing. Try to find out the most effective combination of colors and make lovely cards.

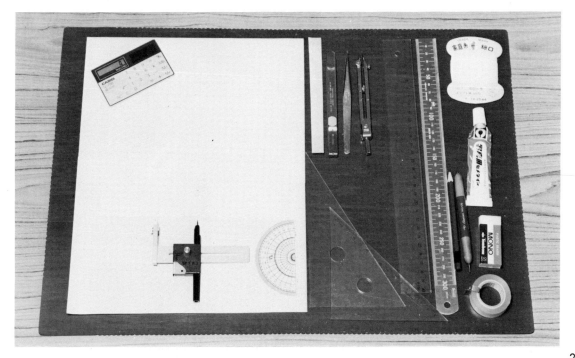

Step-by-step Instructions for Basic Patterns

1. London Bridge, shown on page 6.

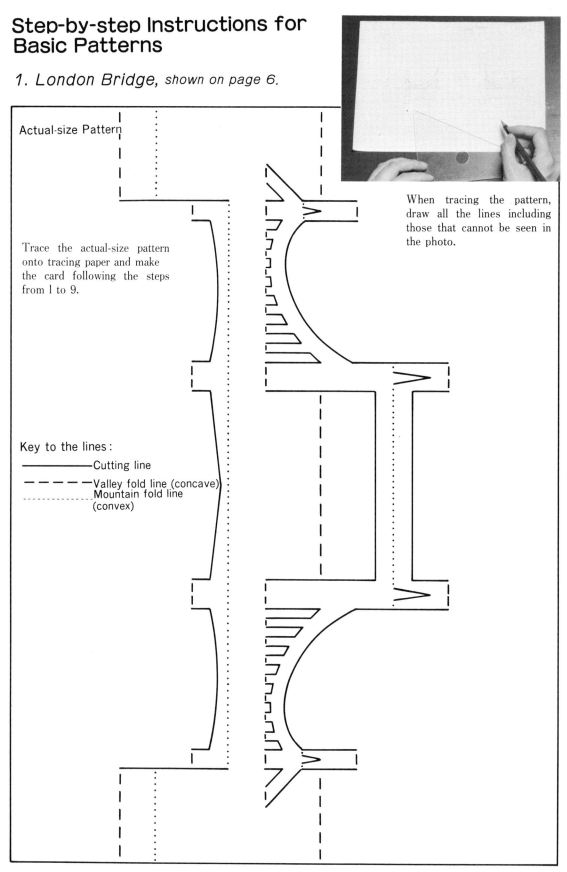

Actual-size Pattern

Trace the actual-size pattern onto tracing paper and make the card following the steps from 1 to 9.

When tracing the pattern, draw all the lines including those that cannot be seen in the photo.

Key to the lines :

——————Cutting line

— — — —Valley fold line (concave)
·············Mountain fold line (convex)

1. When you make your original card, draw your design on graph paper to make a sample. Check whether the sample works well. If not, correct the wrong points until you can get the desired effects. Then make a card using the corrected sample as a pattern.

2. Let's make a "London Bridge" card using the actual-size pattern. Place a sheet of Kent paper on the working board and place the traced pattern on it. Perforate along the pattern with a stylus pen.

3. The pattern is transferred as shown. (Negative picture is used here to show the perforated pattern.)

4. Draw necessary lines with a pencil along holes. Then cut along cutting lines with a cutting knife and a steel ruler.

5. Fold along fold lines.

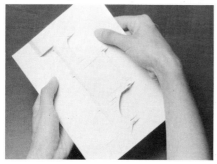

6. All the fold lines are folded.

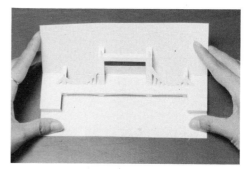

7. Prepare another sheet of Kent paper of the same size (20cm by 15cm) (8"×6") for backing. Fold the Kent paper in half with right sides facing. Apply glue onto the back of the finished card.

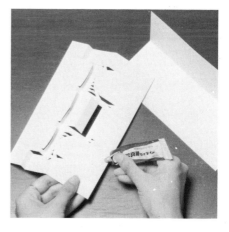

8. Place the glued card onto the backing.

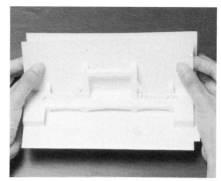

9. Finished card.

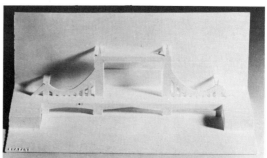

2. Form A, *shown on page 8.*

Key to the lines

———————— Cutting line

— — — — — Valley fold line (concave)

·············· Mountain fold line (convex)

Actual-size
Pattern

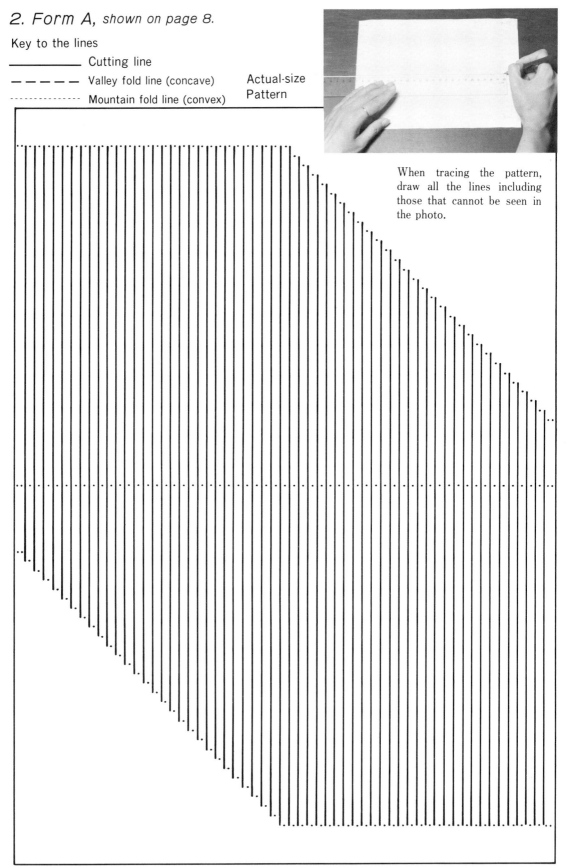

When tracing the pattern, draw all the lines including those that cannot be seen in the photo.

1. Place the traced pattern on a sheet of Kent paper and perforate along the pattern with a stylus pen.

2. The pattern is transferred as shown. (Negative picture is used here to show the perforated pattern.)

3. Score along fold lines and cut along cutting lines with a cutting knife.

4. Begin folding the center line, then fold the top and bottom lines.

5. After creasing, unfold the form. Apply glue onto the top and bottom areas.

6. Make sure to glue evenly. Prepare another sheet of Kent paper (20cm by 15cm) (8" × 6") for the base.

7. Place one side of glued form on the base.

8. After fixing one side, place the other side on the base ane fix.

9. When it is completely dry, open the card. Finished card.

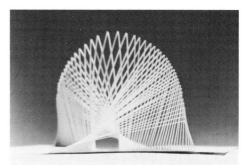

3. New Year's Pine Decoration, *shown on page 10.*

1. Place the actual-size pattern of the pine decoration on a sheet of Kent paper and perforate along the pattern. (Negative picture is used here to show the perforated pattern.)

2. Cut between holes using a cutting knife and a steel ruler.

Actual-size Pattern for Pine Trees.

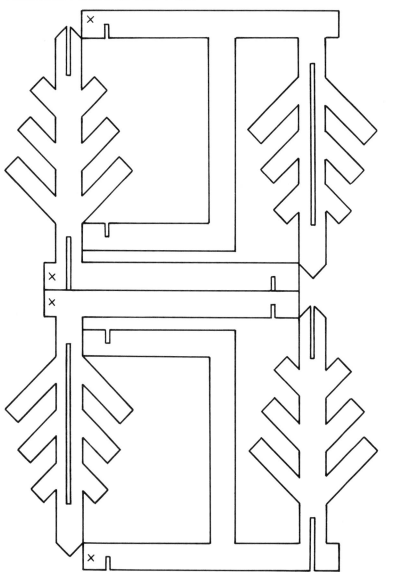

3. All the pieces are cut out. Make sure that all the cutting lines are cut correctly.

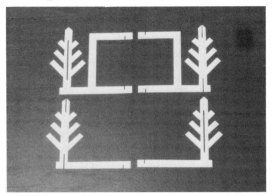

4. Assemble the pieces matching the slits.

Place for Pine Decoration

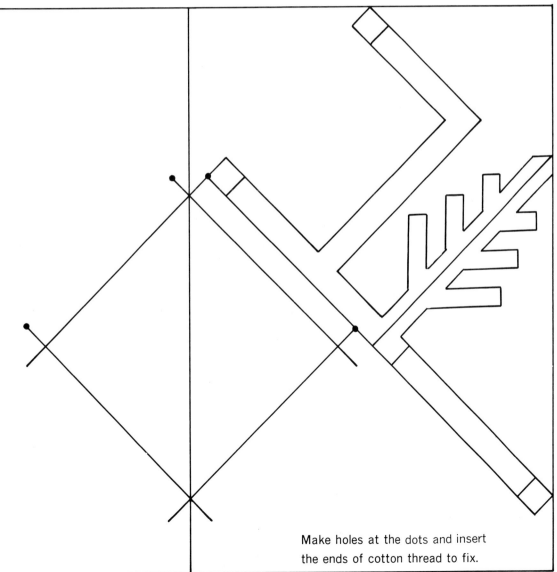

Make holes at the dots and insert the ends of cotton thread to fix.

5. Apply glue to 4 small pieces of Japanese rice paper. Place the end of a cotton thread (6-7cm $(2\,\frac{3}{8}'' - 2\,\frac{3}{4}'')$ long) on each glued paper and attach to the back of the assembled pine decoration.

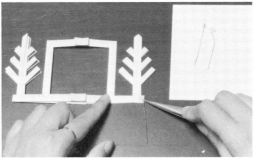

6. Make a base. Place two sheets of 10 cm by 15cm $(4'' \times 6'')$ Kent paper side by side and join with glued Japanese rice paper at the center.

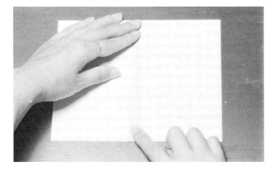

7. Fold the glued paper using the corner of a desk.

8. When opened, you can see the groove at the center of the base.

9. Place the unfolded pattern on the base and perforate the indicated places with a stylus pen.

10. Insert the ends of thread into the holes in the base with pointed tweezers. Loosely pull each end of thread and fix it temporarily with clear adhesive tape.

11. Open the card and check whether the assembled pine decoration pops up.

12. Pull the thread if necessary and glue onto two sheets of 10cm by 15cm $(4'' \times 6'')$ Kent paper for another backing.

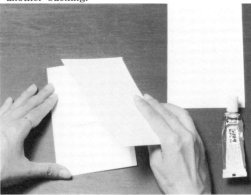

Instructions and Actual-size Patterns

Big Ben,

shown on page 6.

Key to the lines :

———————— Cutting line

— — — — — Valley fold line
(concave)

·············· Mountain fold
line (convex)

18.5
$(7\frac{3}{8}'')$

When tracing the pattern, make sure to add the omitted part of the pattern (11.5cm $(4\frac{5}{8}'')$ $(4\frac{5}{8}''))$.

11.5

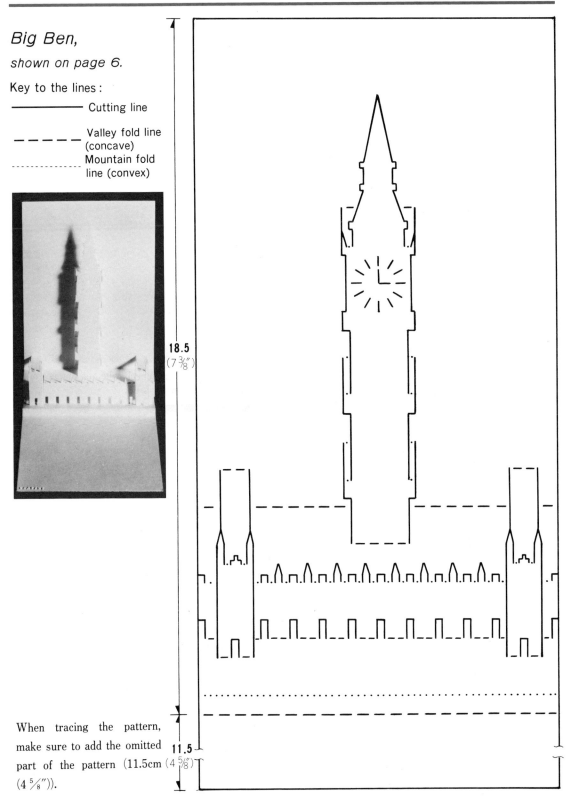

Twin Peaks, *shown on page 12.*

Key to the lines :

——————— Cutting line

— — — — — Valley fold line (concave)

················ Mountain fold line (convex)

Montage A, *shown on page 12.*

Key to the lines :

———————— Cutting line

— — — — — Valley fold line (concave)

············· Mountain fold line (convex)

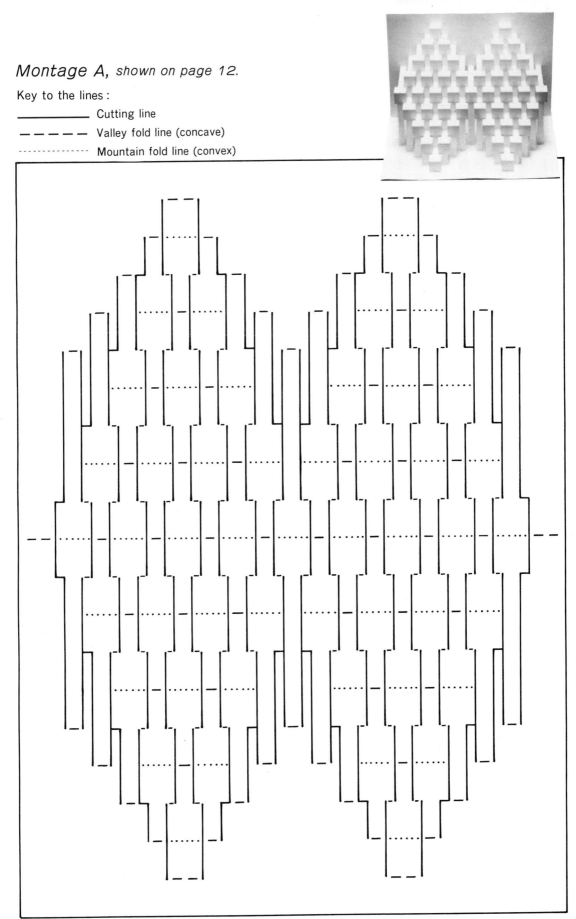

Jungle-gym, *shown on page 13.*

Key to the lines :

─────────── Cutting line

─ ─ ─ ─ ─ Valley fold line (concave)

·············· Mountain fold line (convex)

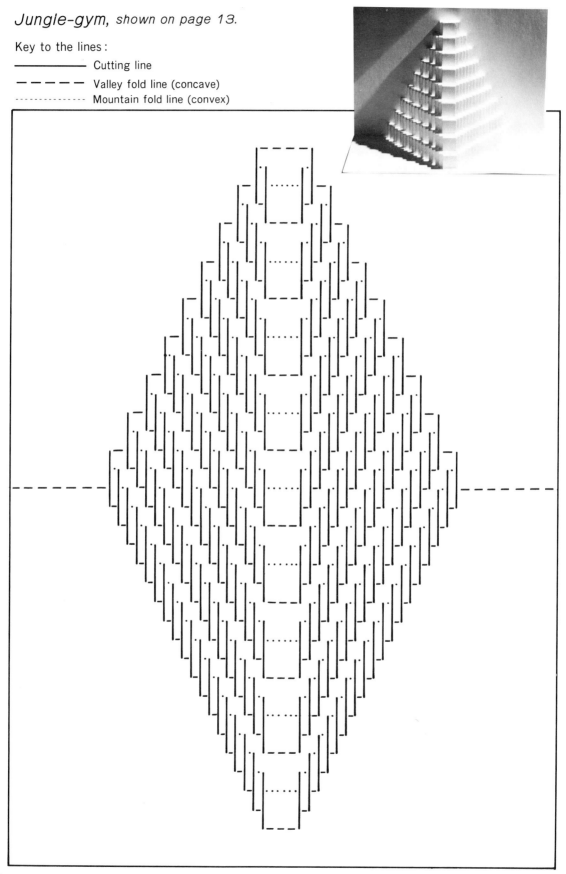

Tumbling Blocks, *shown on page 13.*

Key to the lines :

———————— Cutting line

– – – – – – Valley fold line (concave)

·············· Mountain fold line (convex)

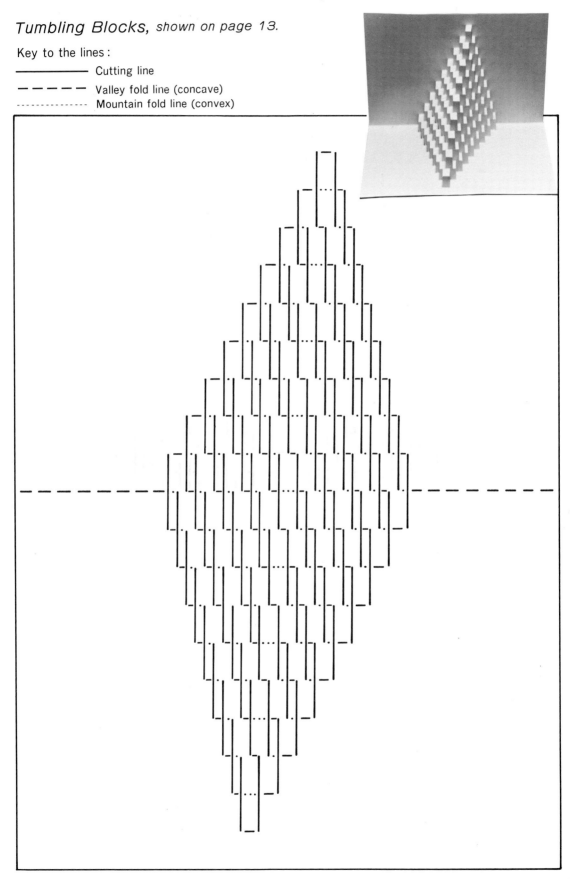

Stairs to Paradise A, *shown on page 14.*

Key to the lines:

———————— Cutting line

— — — — — Valley fold line (concave)

············· Mountain fold line (convex)

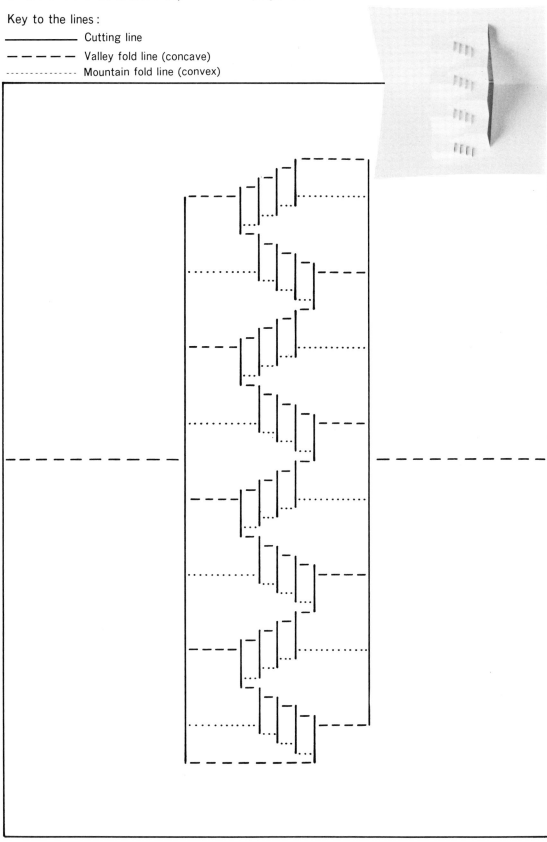

Stairs to Paradise B, *shown on page 14.*

Key to the lines :

————————— Cutting line

— — — — — Valley fold line (concave)

·················· Mountain fold line (convex)

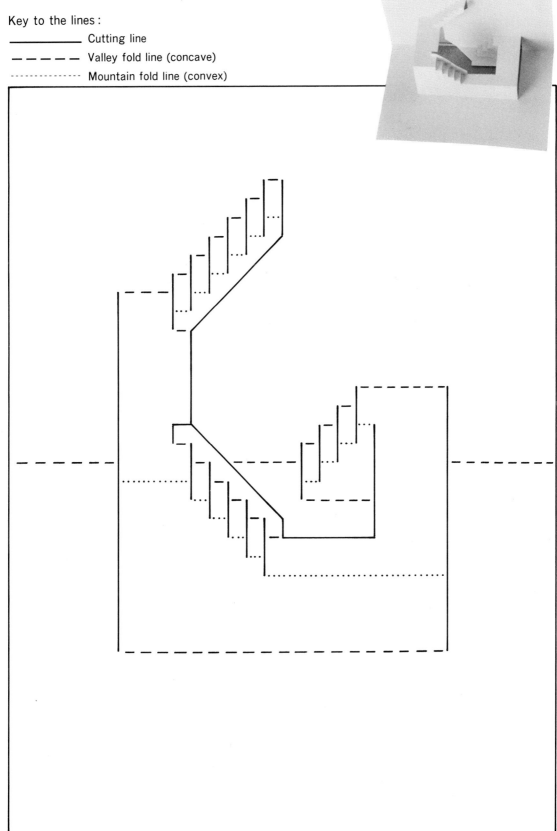

Stairs Paradise C, *shown on page 15.*

Key to the lines :

———————— Cutting line

— — — — — Valley fold line (concave)

---------------- Mountain fold line (convex)

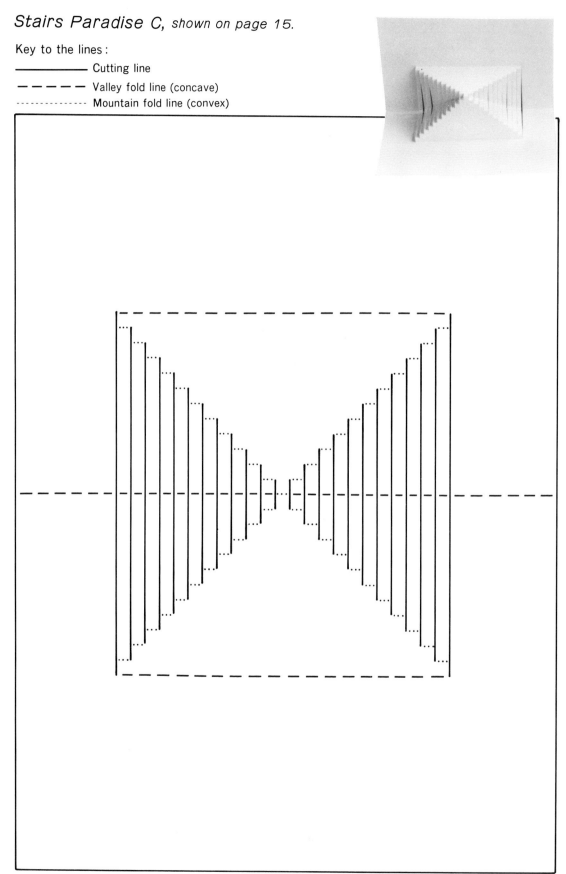

Stairs to Paradise E, *shown on page 15.*

Key to the lines:

——————— Cutting line

— — — — — Valley fold line (concave)

-------------- Mountain fold line (convex)

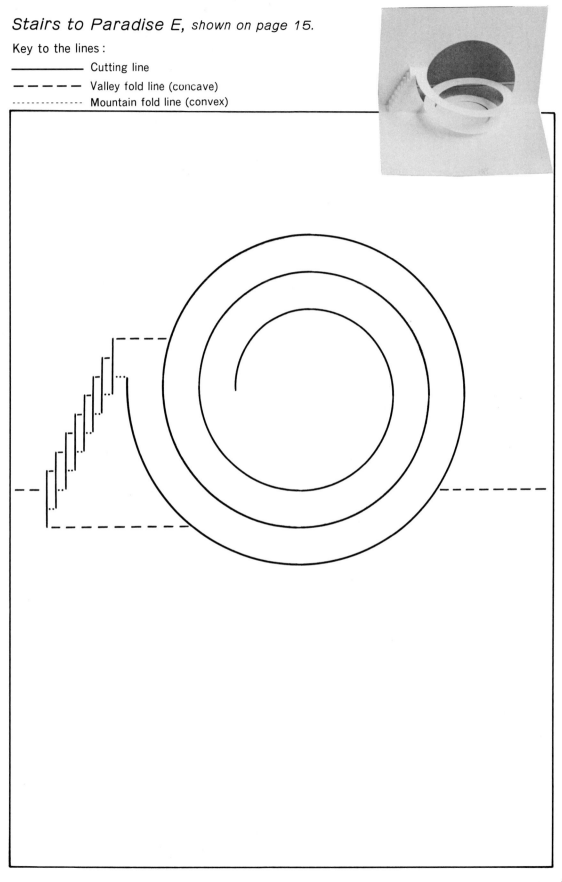

Chairs A, *shown on page 16.*

Key to the lines:

——————— Cutting line

— — — — — Valley fold line (concave)

·············· Mountain fold line (convex)

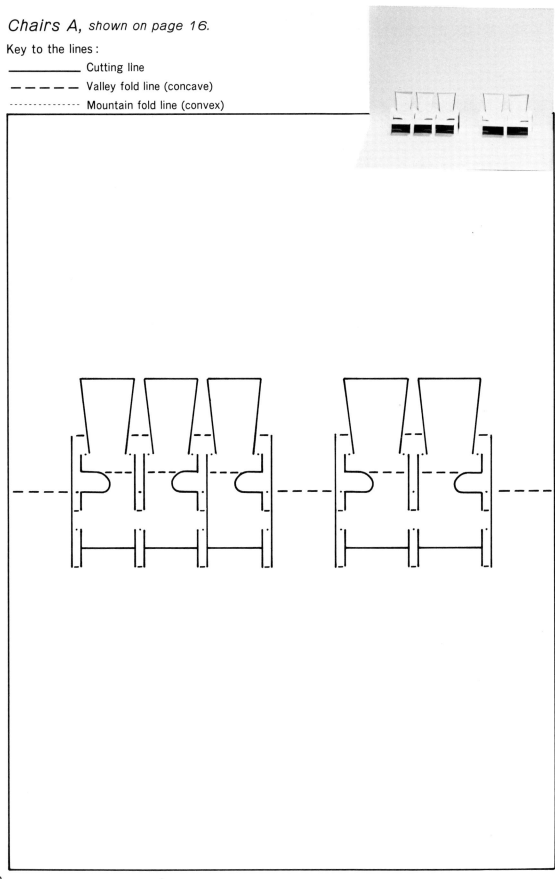

Chairs B, *shown on page 16.*

Key to the lines :

——————— Cutting line

— — — — — Valley fold line (concave)

------------- Mountain fold line (convex)

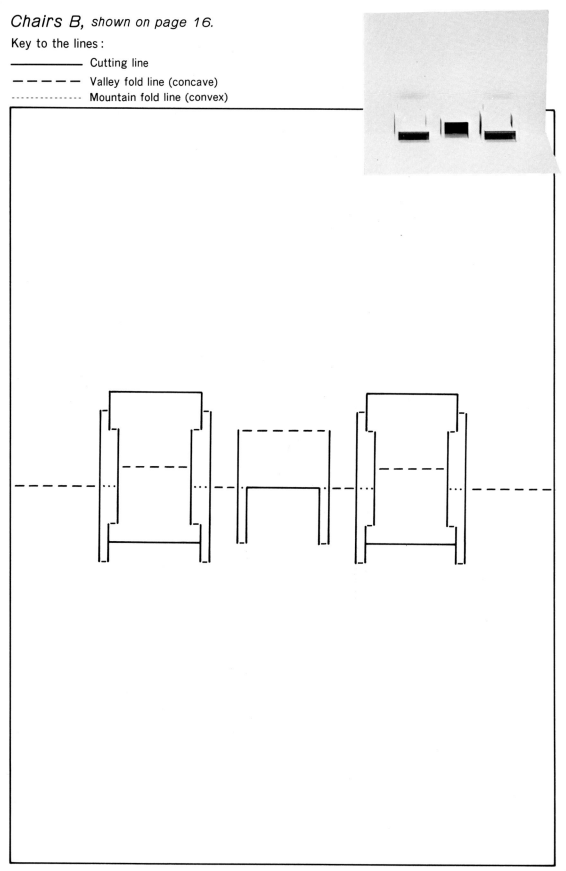

Dresser,
shown on page 16.

Key to the lines :

———————— Cutting line

— — — — — Valley fold line (concave)

·············· Mountain fold line (convex)

15
(6″)

15
(6″)

●Make the upper half same size
as the lower half.

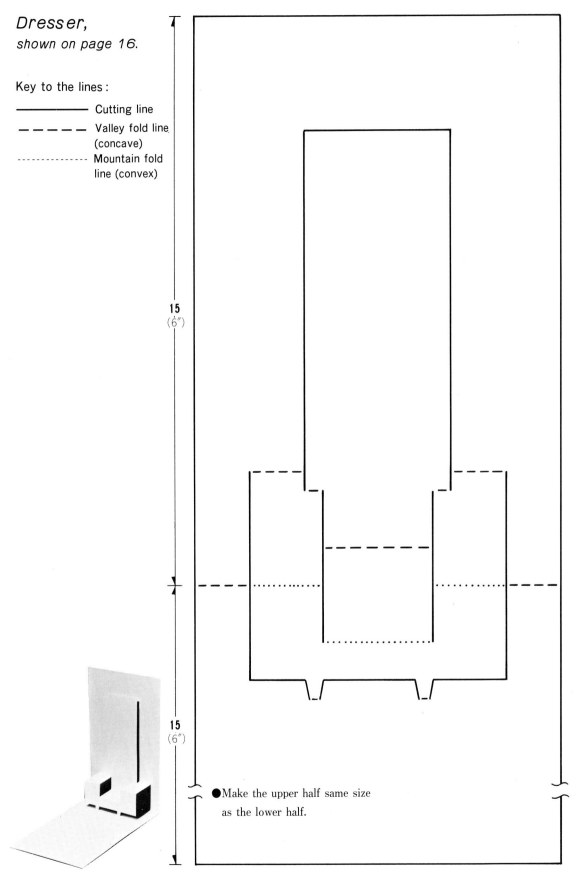

44

Beds, *shown on page 16.*

Key to the lines :

—————— Cutting line

– – – – – Valley fold line (concave)

·············· Mountain fold line (convex)

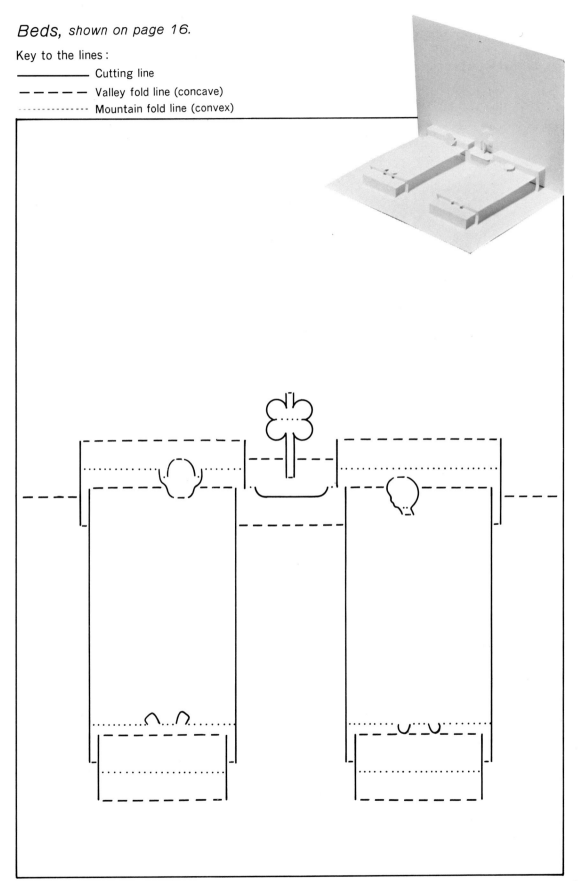

Children's Room, *shown on page 17.*

Key to the lines :

————— Cutting line

— — — — — Valley fold line (concave)

············· Mountain fold line (convex)

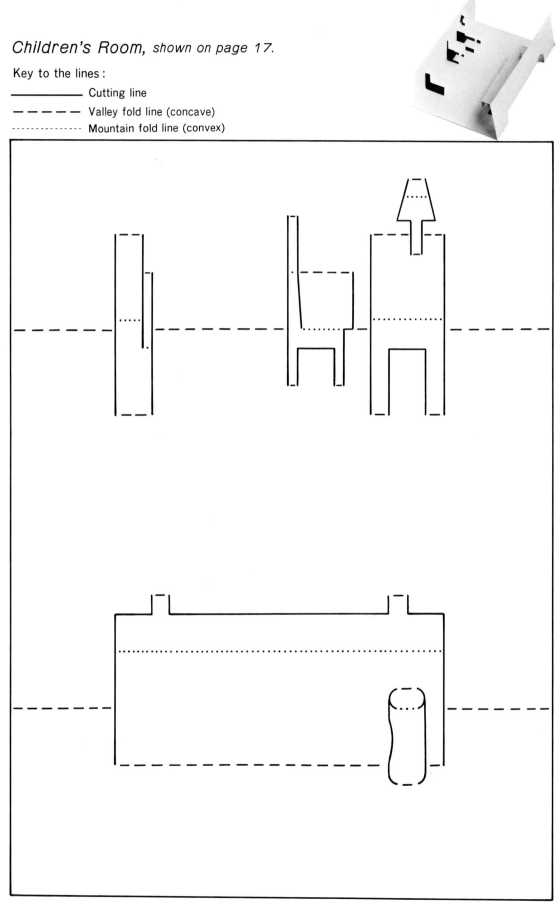

Steam Locomotive, *shown on page 18.*

Key to the lines :

———————— Cutting line

— — — — — Valley fold line (concave)

·············· Mountain fold line (convex)

Passenger Car, *shown on page 18.*

Key to the lines :

————————— Cutting line

— — — — — Valley fold line (concave)

·············· Mountain fold line (convex)

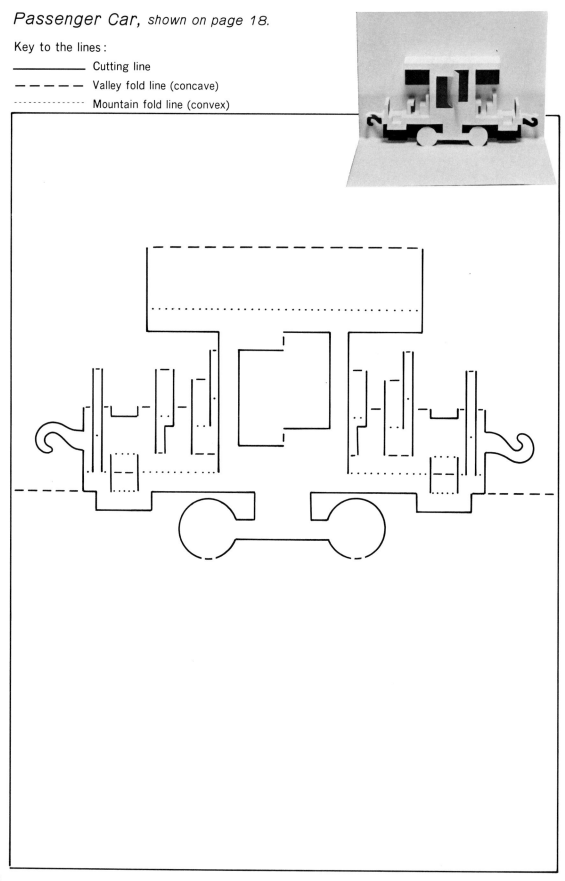

Sailboat A, *shown on page 19.*

Key to the lines :

_____ Cutting line

_ _ _ _ _ _ Valley fold line (concave)

.... Mountain fold line (convex)

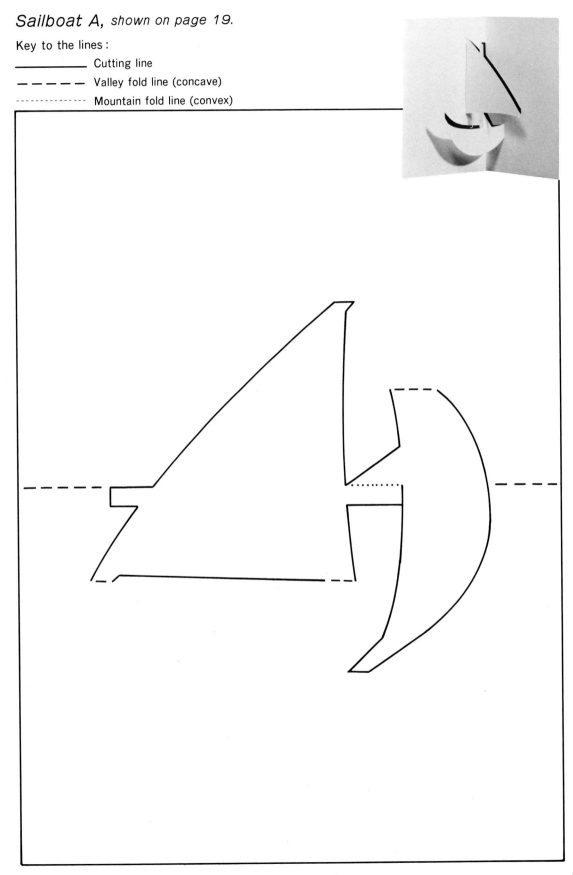

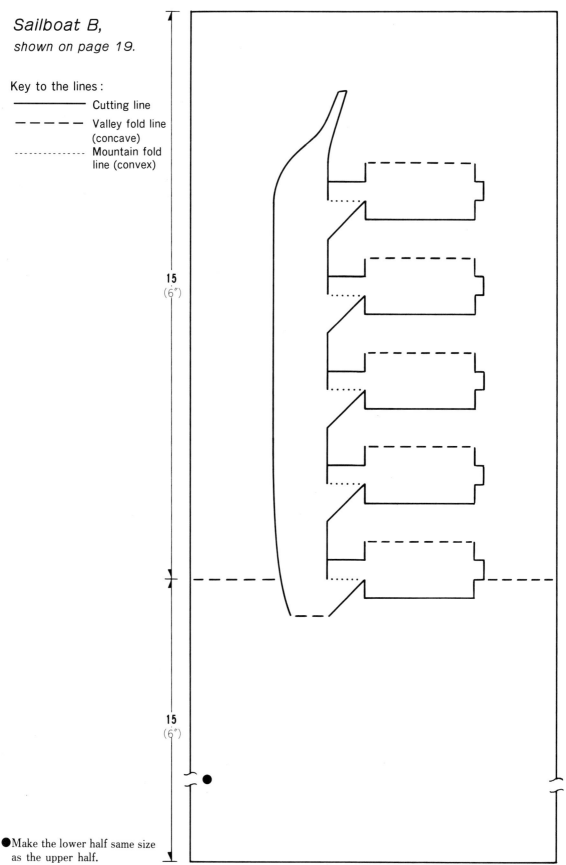

Sailboat B,
shown on page 19.

Key to the lines :
——————— Cutting line
— — — — — Valley fold line
(concave)
·············· Mountain fold
line (convex)

15
(6″)

15
(6″)

●Make the lower half same size
as the upper half.

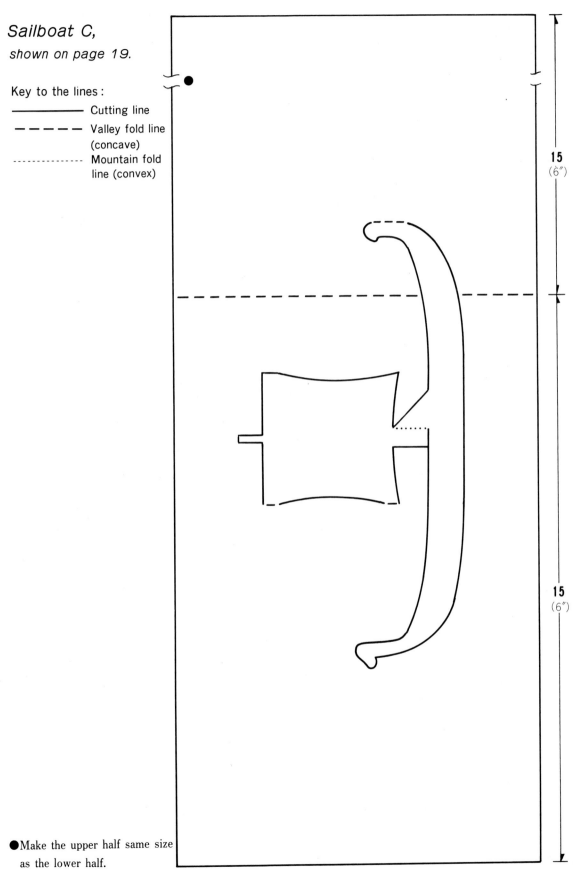

Sailboat C,
shown on page 19.

Key to the lines :

———————— Cutting line

– – – – – Valley fold line
(concave)

·············· Mountain fold
line (convex)

15
(6″)

15
(6″)

●Make the upper half same size
as the lower half.

Circular Construction A, *shown on page 20.*

Key to the lines :

——————— Cutting line

— — — — — Valley fold line (concave)

·············· Mountain fold line (convex)

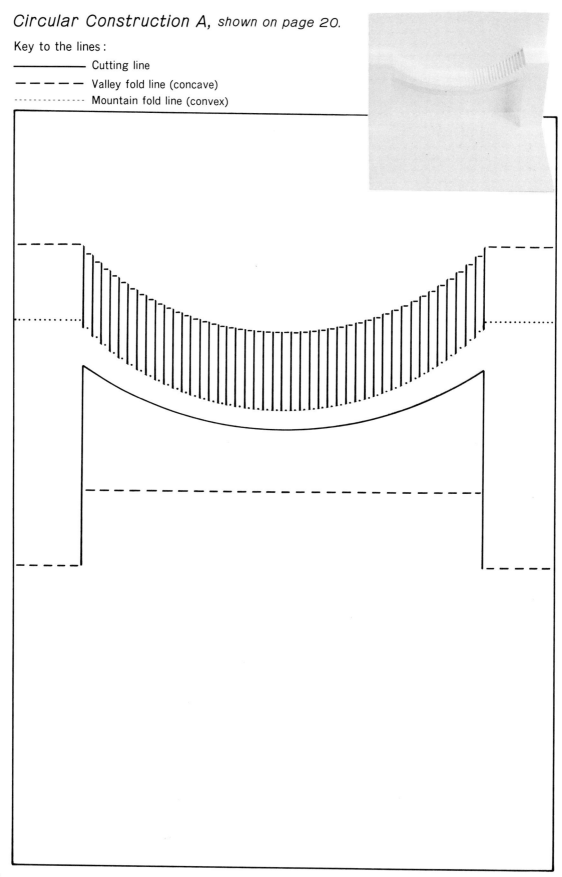

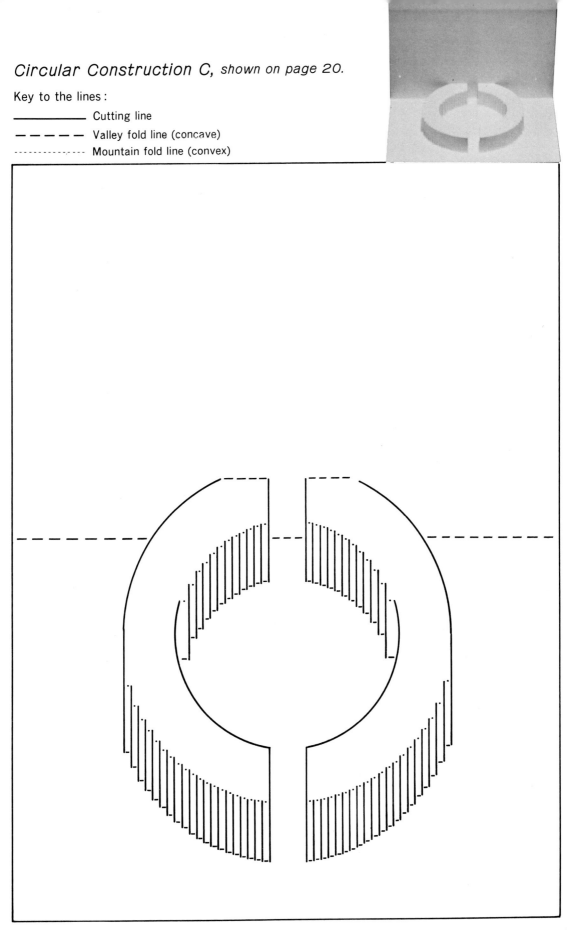

Circular Construction C, *shown on page 20.*

Key to the lines :

——————— Cutting line

— — — — — Valley fold line (concave)

------------- Mountain fold line (convex)

Double Arch Bridge, *shown on page 21.*

Key to the lines :

————————— Cutting line

— — — — — Valley fold line (concave)

·············· Mountain fold line (convex)

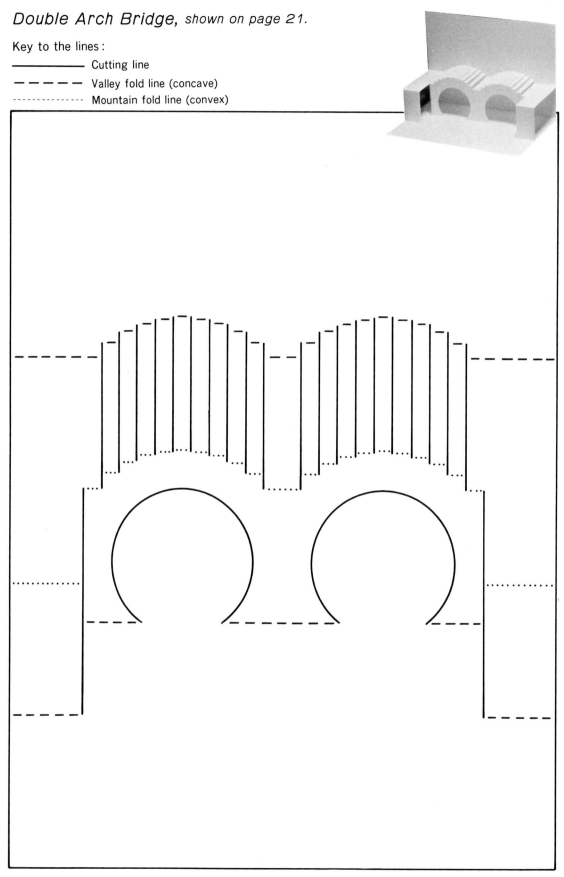

Shinto Shrine Archway,
shown on page 21.

Key to the lines :

————————— Cutting line

— — — — — Valley fold line (concave)

·············· Mountain fold line (convex)

Actual-size Patterns (Cut two pieces each.)

Actual-size Pattern for the Base

Cut out two pieces each of stands and archway and glue them together with the end of a thread in between. Assemble stands and archway at right angles. Insert end of thread into the indicated hole.

● Make the lower half same size as the upper half.

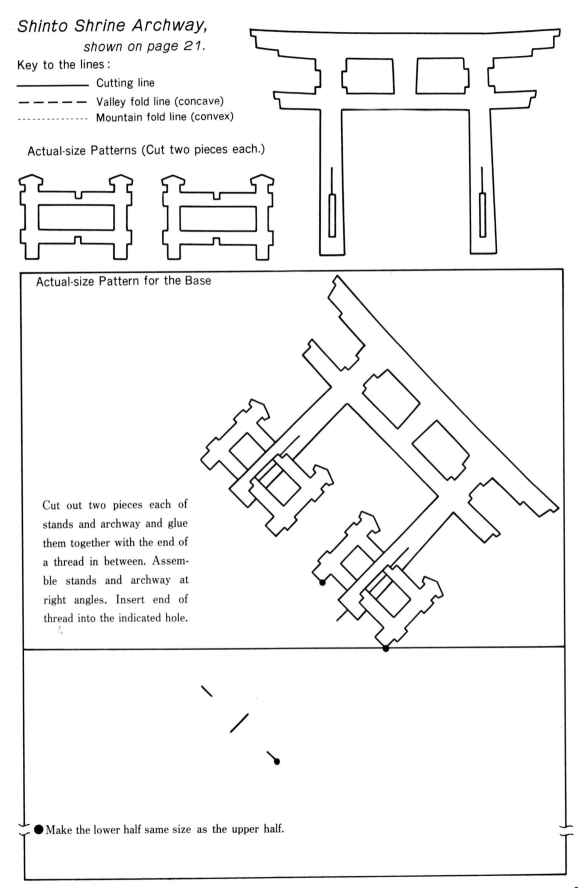

Cutlery Set, *shown on page 22.*

Key to the lines :

———————— Cutting line

— — — — — Valley fold line (concave)

·············· Mountain fold line (convex)

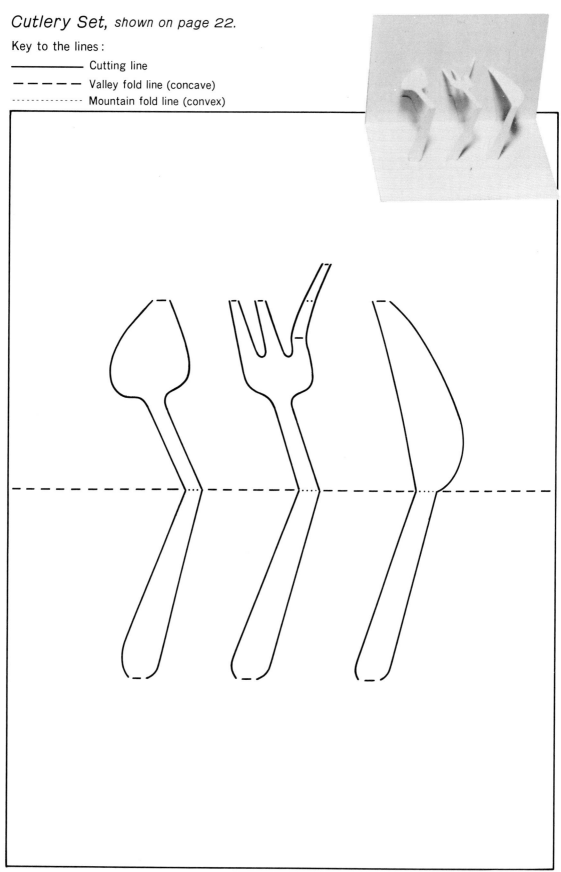

Comb, *shown on page 22.*

Key to the lines :

———————— Cutting line

— — — — — Valley fold line (concave)

------------------ Mountain fold line (convex)

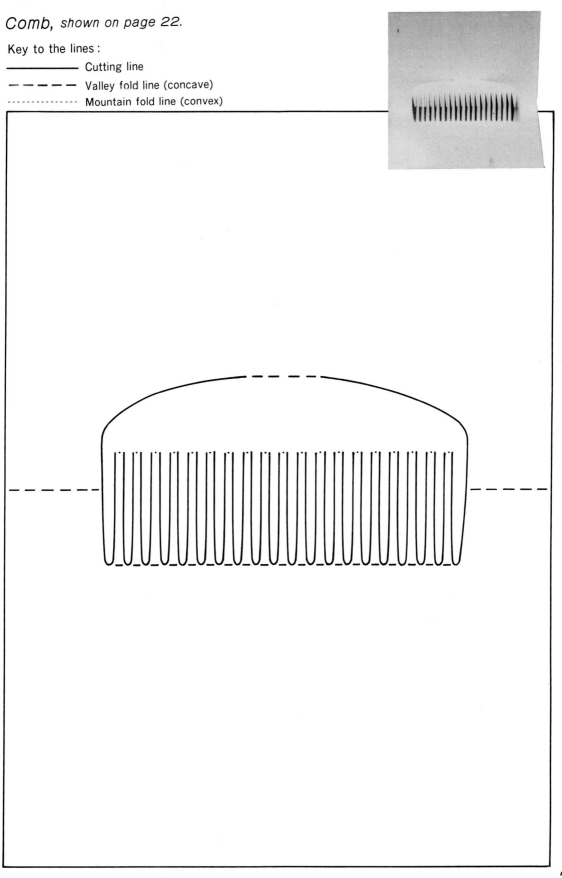

Bowl and Chopsticks, *shown on page 22.*

Key to the lines:

─────────── Cutting line

─ ─ ─ ─ ─ Valley fold line (concave)

·············· Mountain fold line (convex)

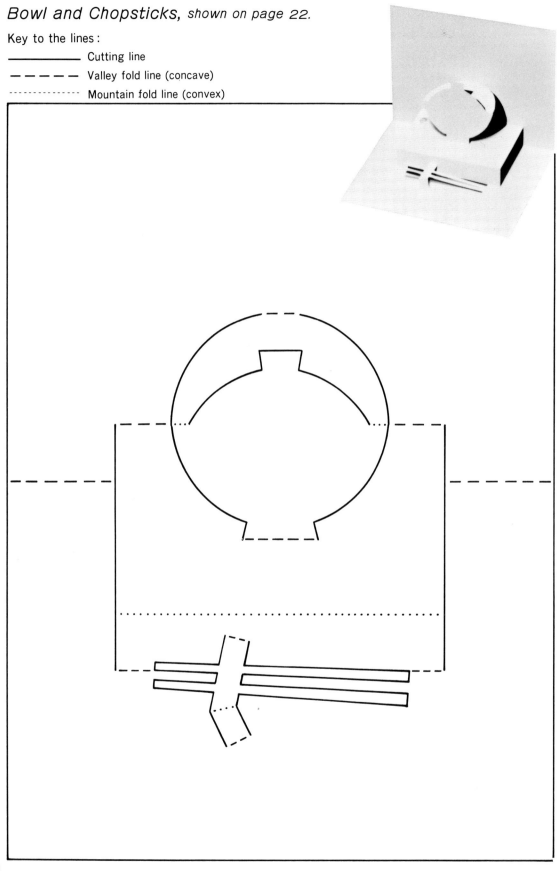

Bon Voyage, shown on page 23.

Key to the lines :

──────────── Cutting line

── ── ── ── Valley fold line (concave)

·············· Mountain fold line (convex)

Thank you, *shown on page 23.*

Key to the lines :

———————— Cutting line

— — — — — Valley fold line (concave)

-------------- Mountain fold line (convex)

Au revoir, shown on page 23.

Key to the lines :

———————— Cutting line

— — — — — Valley fold line (concave)

·················· Mountain fold line (convex)

Bonus, *shown on page 23.*

Key to the lines :

──────── Cutting line

– – – – – Valley fold line (concave)

·············· Mountain fold line (convex)

"Peace" & *"I love you"*, *shown on page 23.*

Key to the lines :

——————— Cutting line

– – – – – Valley fold line (concave)

·············· Mountain fold line (convex)

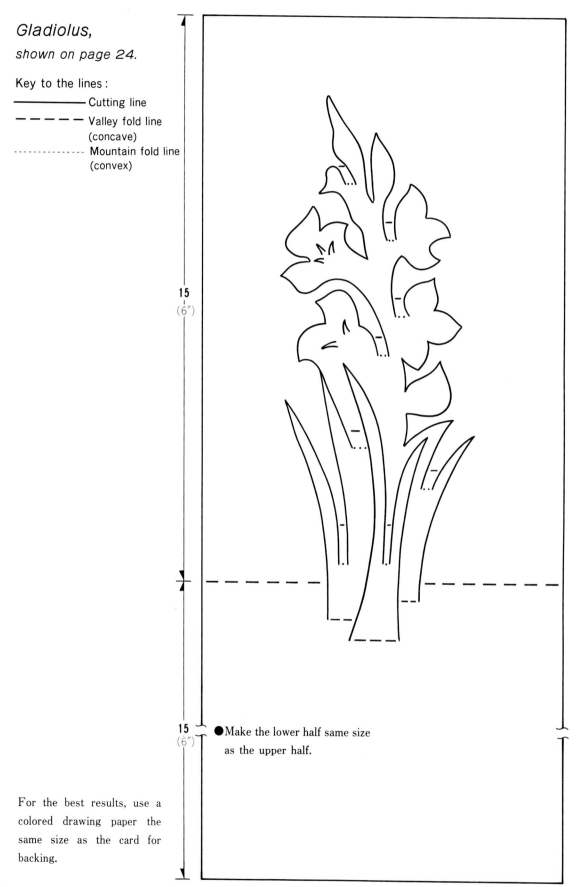

Gladiolus,

shown on page 24.

Key to the lines :

——————— Cutting line

— — — — — Valley fold line
(concave)

·············· Mountain fold line
(convex)

15
(6″)

15
(6″)

● Make the lower half same size
as the upper half.

For the best results, use a
colored drawing paper the
same size as the card for
backing.

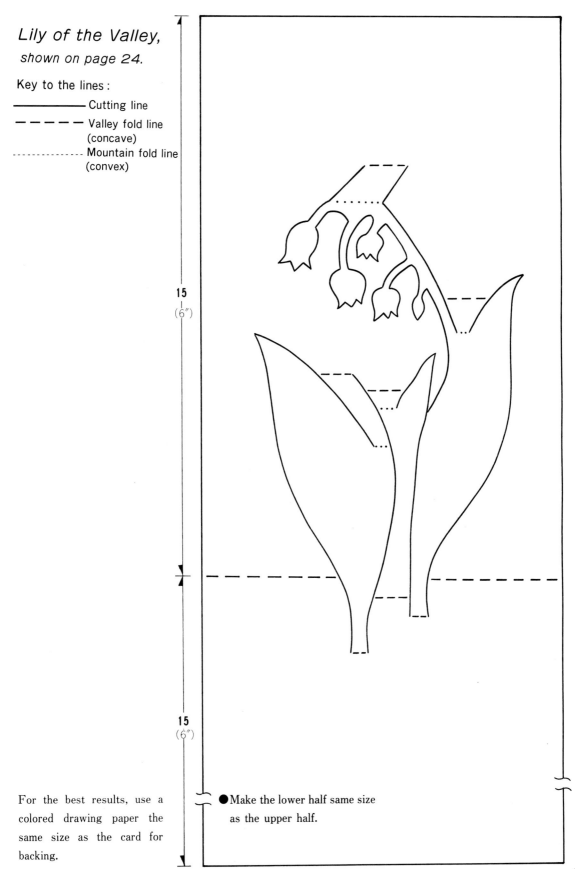

Lily of the Valley,
shown on page 24.

Key to the lines :

———————— Cutting line

— — — — — Valley fold line
(concave)

------------- Mountain fold line
(convex)

15
(6″)

15
(6″)

For the best results, use a
colored drawing paper the
same size as the card for
backing.

● Make the lower half same size
as the upper half.

Rose, shown on page 24.

Key to the lines :

──────── Cutting line

─ ─ ─ ─ ─ Valley fold line
(concave)

·············· Mountain fold line
(convex)

15
(6″)

15
(6″)

●Make the lower half same size
as the upper half.

For the best results, use a
colored drawing paper the
same size as the card for
backing.

Hibiscus, *shown on page 24.*

Key to the lines :

───────── Cutting line

─ ─ ─ ─ ─ Valley fold line (concave)

- - - - - - - - - Mountain fold line (convex)

For the best results, use a colored drawing paper the same
size as the card for backing.

Dahlia, *shown on page 24.*

Key to the lines :

———————— Cutting line
– – – – – – Valley fold line (concave)
·············· Mountain fold line (convex)

For the best results, use a colored drawing paper the same size as the card for backing.

Azalea, *shown on page 24.*

Key to the lines :

———————— Cutting line

— — — — — Valley fold line (concave)

· · · · · · · · · · · · Mountain fold line (convex)

For the best results, use a colored drawing paper the same
size as the card for backing.

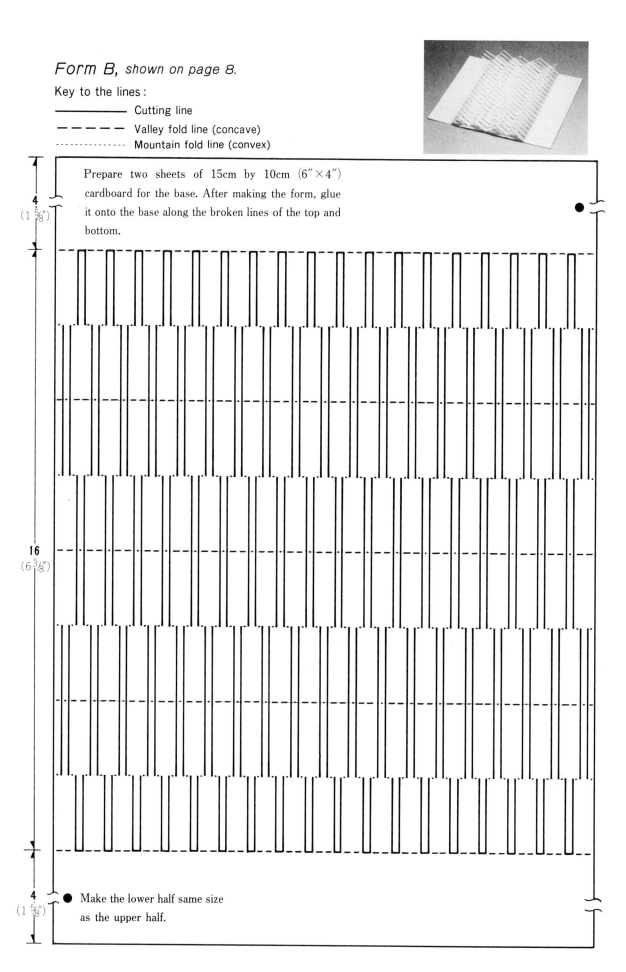

Form B, *shown on page 8.*

Key to the lines :

——————— Cutting line

– – – – – Valley fold line (concave)

················· Mountain fold line (convex)

Prepare two sheets of 15cm by 10cm (6″×4″) cardboard for the base. After making the form, glue it onto the base along the broken lines of the top and bottom.

4
(1 ⅝″)

16
(6 ⅜″)

4
(1 ⅝″)

● Make the lower half same size as the upper half.

Form C, shown on page 9.

Key to the lines :

―――――――― Cutting line

― ― ― ― ― Valley fold line (concave)

·············· Mountain fold line (convex)

Cut along the cutting lines and fold along the fold lines. Apply glue onto semi-circles at top and bottom and place on the 20cm by 15cm (8″×6″) base.

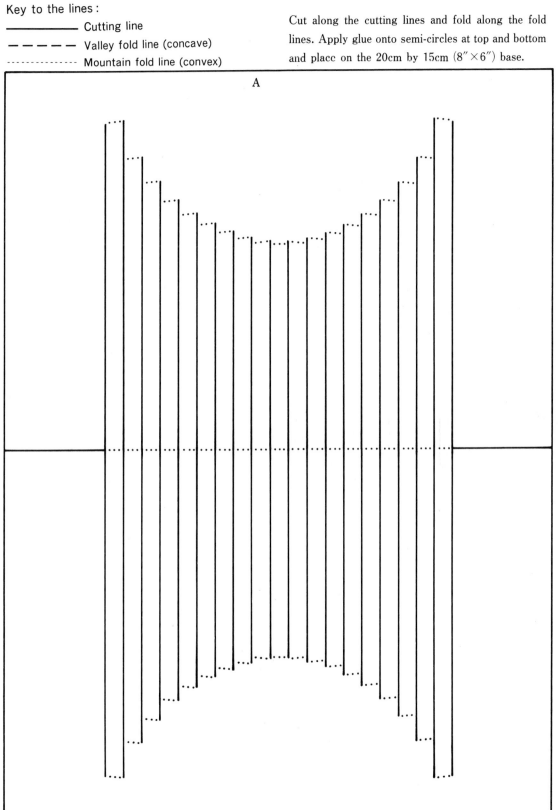

A

B

Form D, *shown on page 9.*

Key to the lines:

——————— Cutting line

– – – – – Valley fold line (concave)

·············· Mountain fold line (convex)

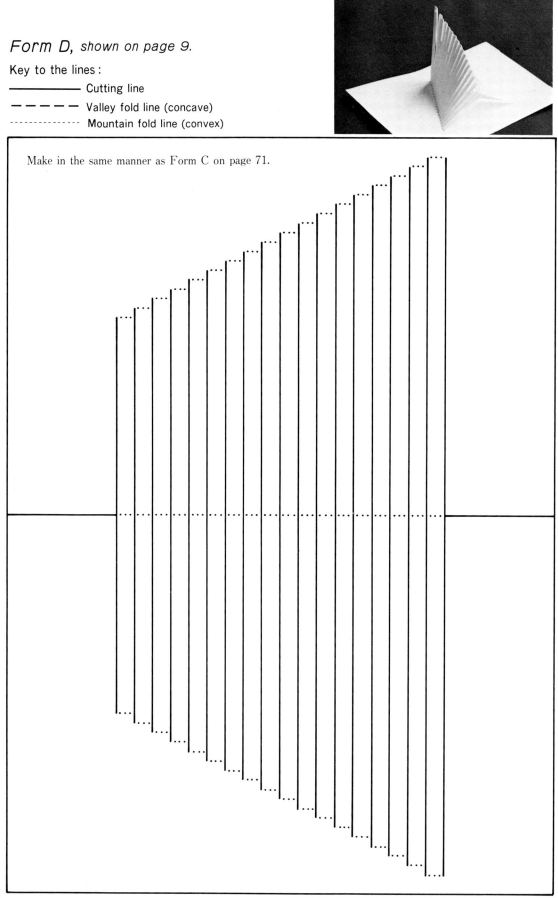

Make in the same manner as Form C on page 71.

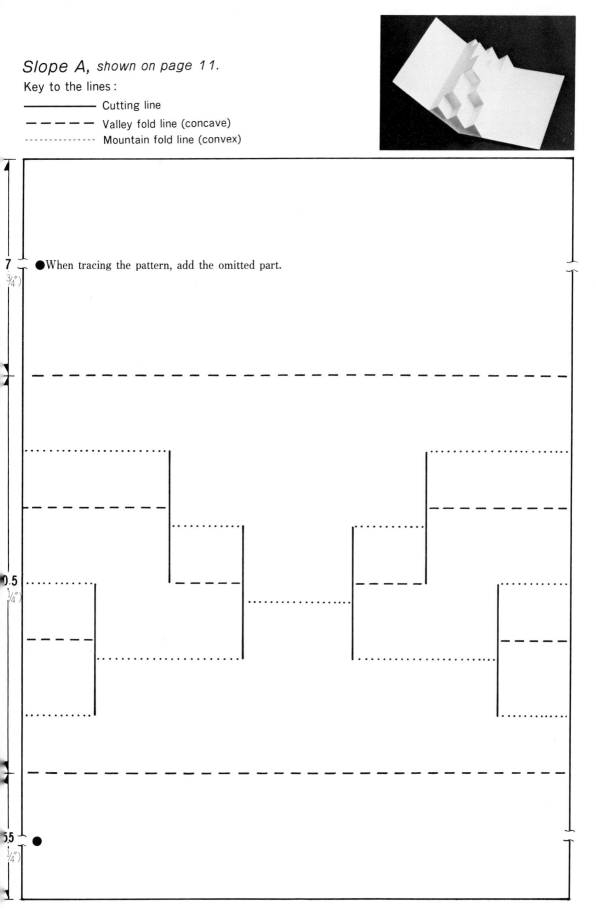

Slope A, *shown on page 11.*

Key to the lines:

───── Cutting line

── ── ── Valley fold line (concave)

·············· Mountain fold line (convex)

●When tracing the pattern, add the omitted part.

7

³⁄₄″)

0.5

¹⁄₄″)

5.5

¹⁄₄″)

House on Stilts, *shown on page 10.*

Actual-size Patterns for the House
Cut one each.

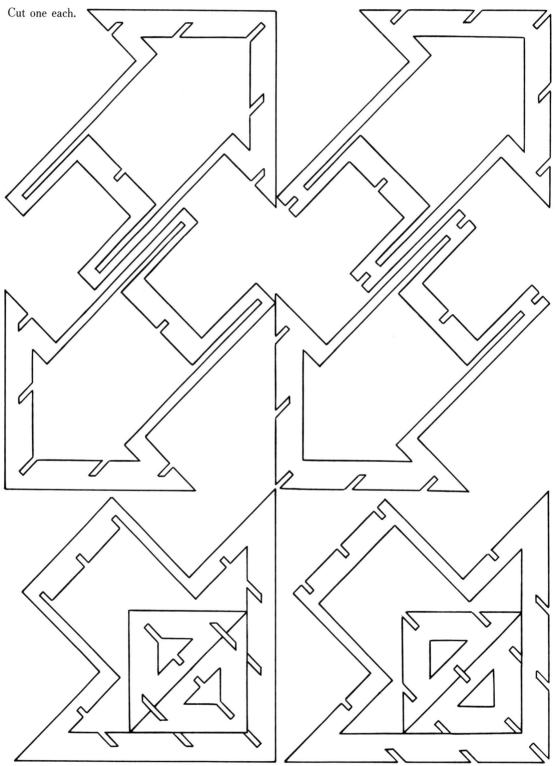

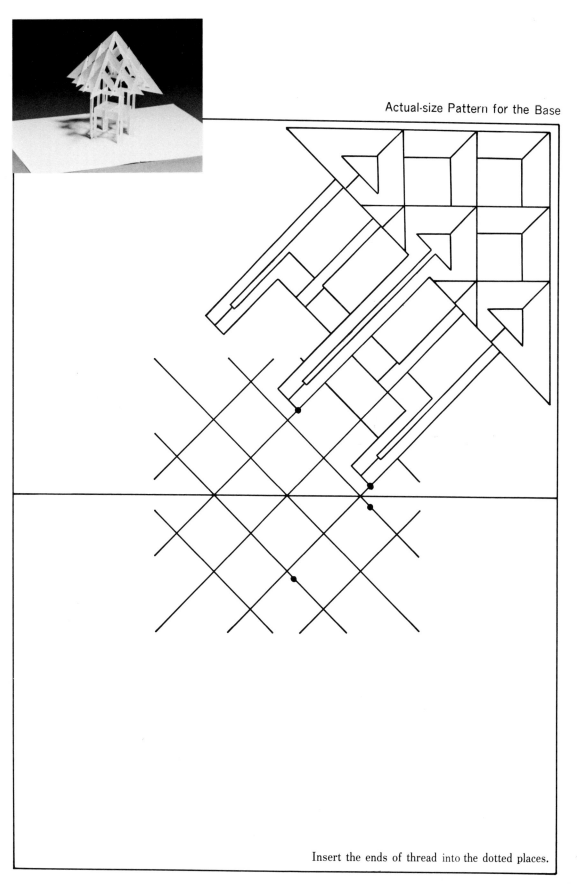

Insert the ends of thread into the dotted places.

Globe, *shown on page 7.*

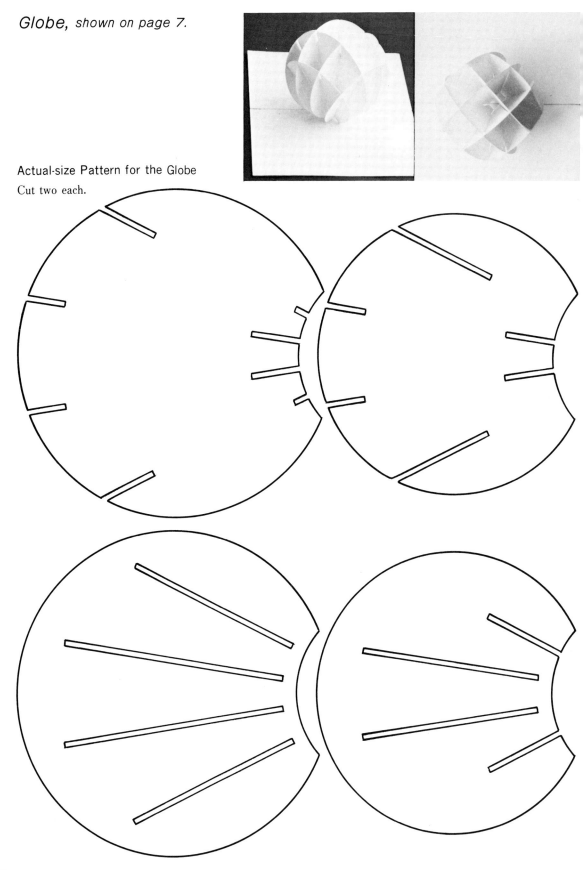

Actual-size Pattern for the Globe
Cut two each.

Actual-size Pattern for the Base

Insert the ends of thread into the dotted places.

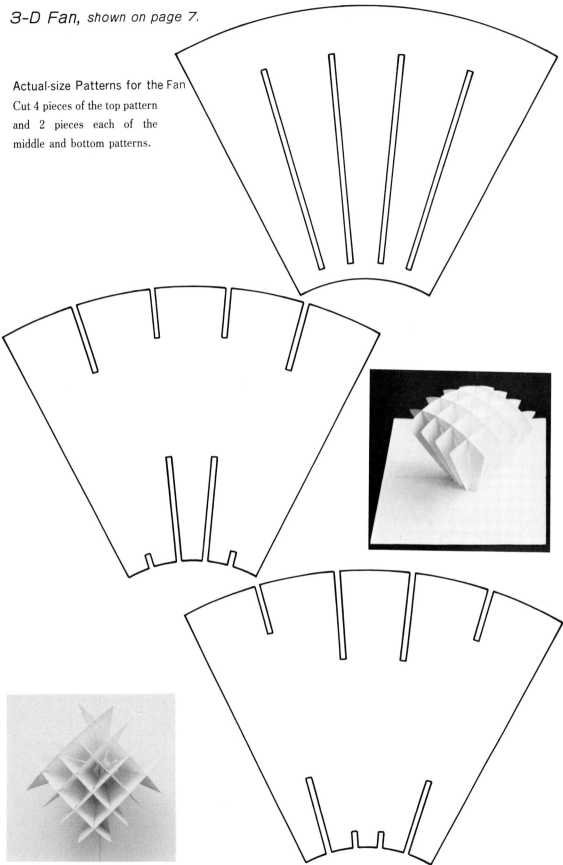

3-D Fan, shown on page 7.

Actual-size Patterns for the Fan
Cut 4 pieces of the top pattern
and 2 pieces each of the
middle and bottom patterns.

Actual-size Pattern for the Base

Insert ends of thread into the dotted places.

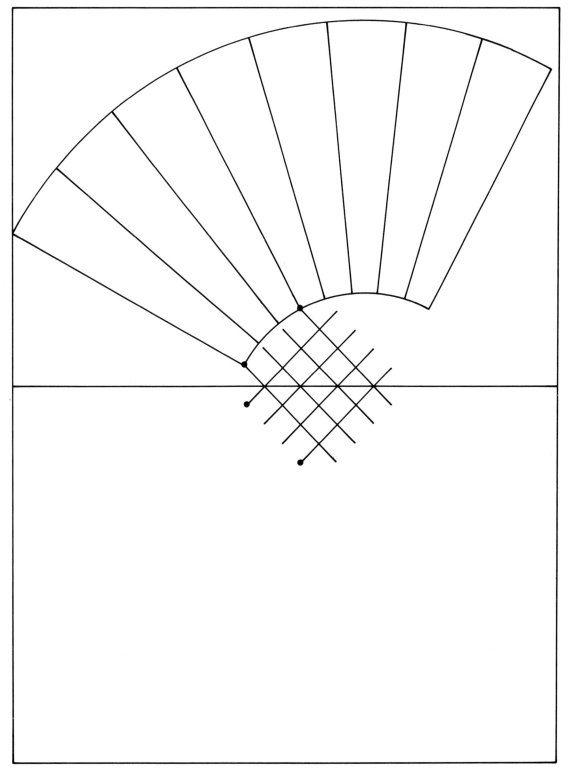

Slope B, *shown on page 11.*

shown on page 11.

Key to the lines :
——————— Cutting line
— — — — — Valley fold line
(concave)
················· Mountain fold line
(convex)

This pattern is reduced.
Enlarge the pattern to the
size indicated.

One sheet of 20cm by
15cm (8″×6″) cardboard
is required for the base in
addition to Kent paper.

8
(3 ¼″)

8
(3 ¼″)

13
(5 ¼″)

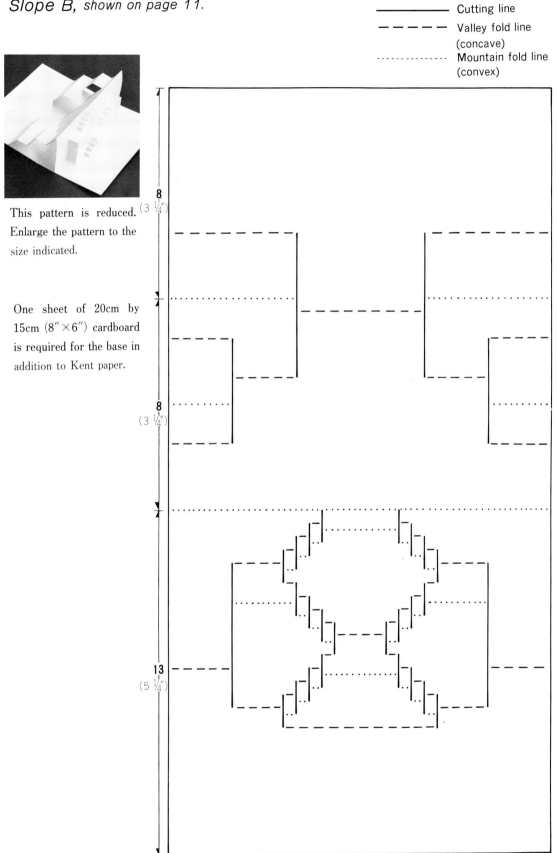

Automobile Pavilion, *shown on page 5.*

Key to the lines :

—————— Cutting line

— — — — — Valley fold line (concave)

·············· Mountain fold line (convex)

Four sheets of 20cm by 15cm (8″×6″) white Kent paper are required to make this card.

Ⓐ Pattern for the Building

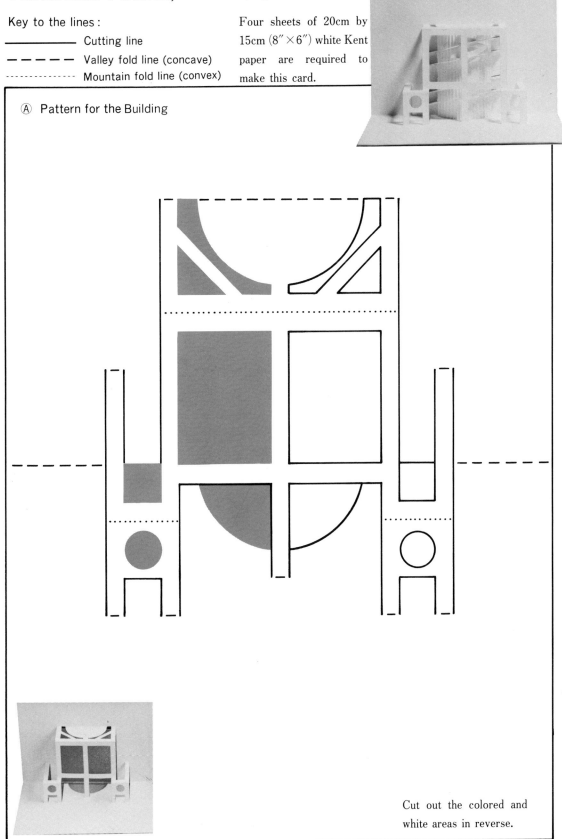

Cut out the colored and white areas in reverse.

Cut and fold pattern D. Then, cut and fold pattern C and assemble four semi-circles. Apply glue on the back of overlapping areas. Cut and fold pattern B and insert into the semi-circles C and D. Attach the decoration in place. Cut and fold pattern A and enclose the above patterns.

Ⓑ Pattern for the Tower

Cut out the colored areas.

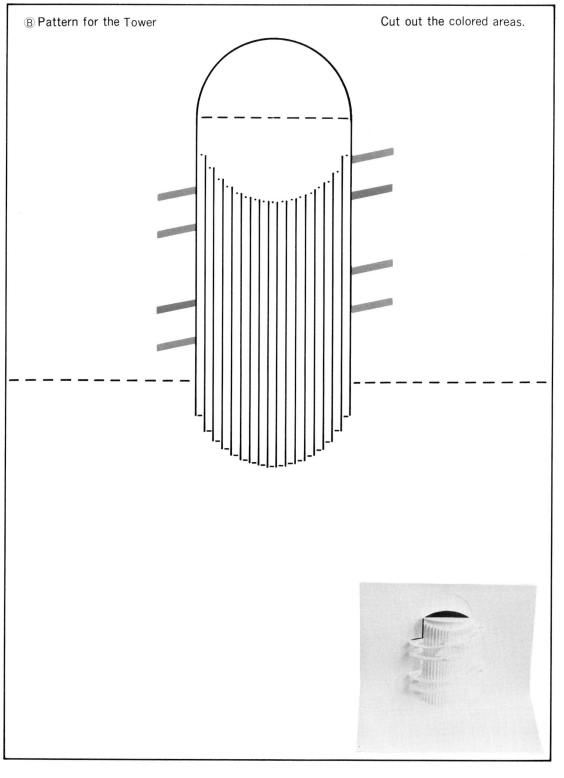

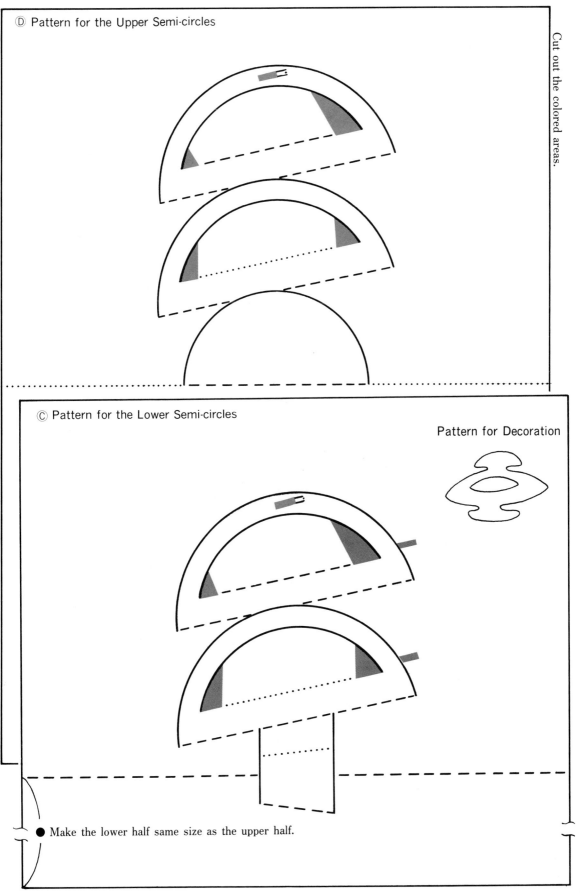

Ⓓ Pattern for the Upper Semi-circles

Ⓒ Pattern for the Lower Semi-circles

Pattern for Decoration

● Make the lower half same size as the upper half.

Sumo Stadium, *shown on page 5.*

Pattern for the Building

Cut out one piece each of parts A to N. Assemble the parts in alphabetical order. First, cross part A and part B, then, parts C, D, E and F, matching slits. Join parts K, L, M, and N to finish. Attach cotton threads to X-marked places of C, D, E and F, using small pieces of Japanese rice paper for joints.

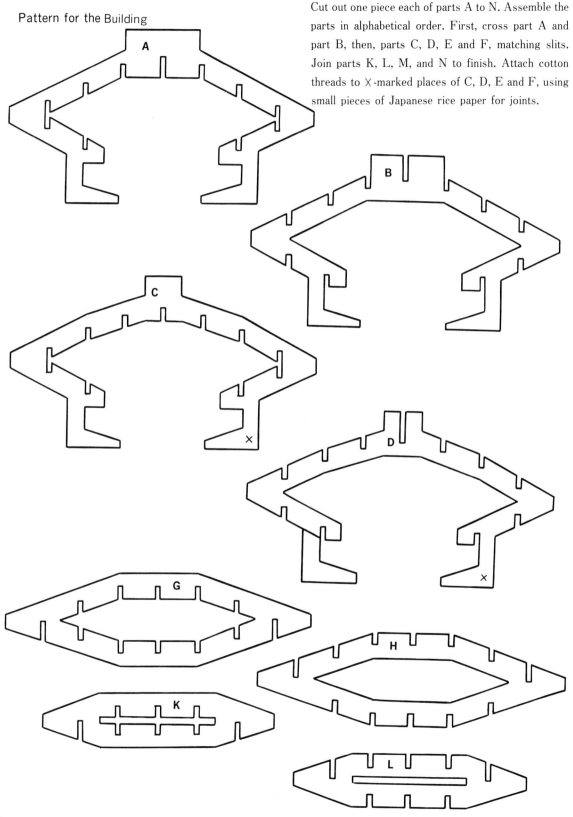

Pattern for the Foundation

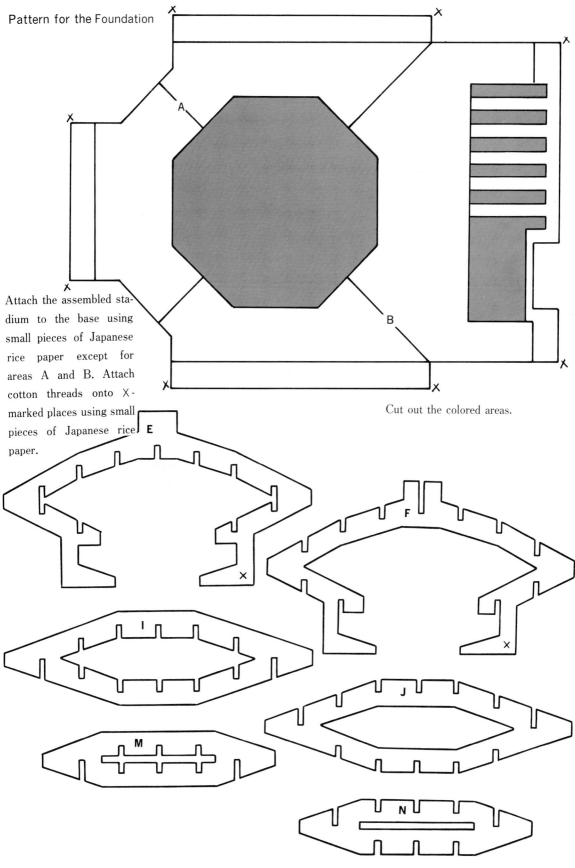

A

B

Attach the assembled stadium to the base using small pieces of Japanese rice paper except for areas A and B. Attach cotton threads onto X-marked places using small pieces of Japanese rice paper.

Cut out the colored areas.

E

F

I

J

M

N

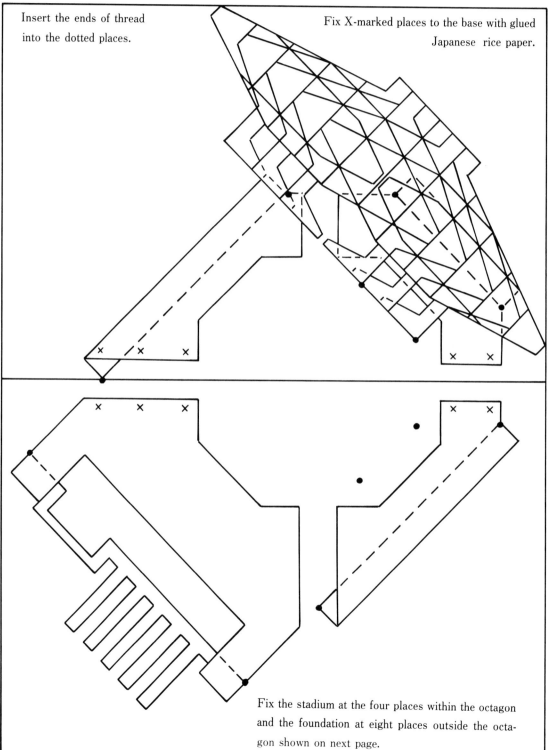

Insert the ends of thread into the dotted places.

Fix X-marked places to the base with glued Japanese rice paper.

Fix the stadium at the four places within the octagon and the foundation at eight places outside the octagon shown on next page.

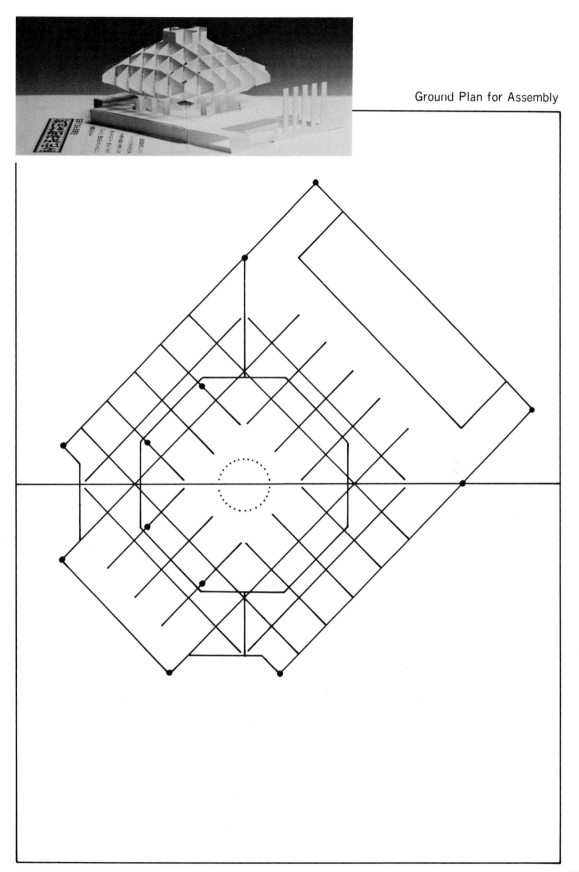

Important Points in Making Pop-up Cards

1. To make the 90° open type card :

The 90° open type cards are made by cutting and folding as indicated. The main points in making the 90° open type cards are as follows :

How to cut the pattern :

Place a traced pattern on a sheet of Kent paper and transfer the pattern by perforating with a stylus pen. Using a cutting knife and a steel ruler, cut along the perforated lines. When cutting a sharp angle, cut each side toward the point. For curves, use a circle cutter or draw curves with a pencil and cut along pencil lines free hand. Make sure that cutting is done exactly along the lines.

How to crease :

A stylus pen is usually used for creasing. For a valley-fold line, score on the right side and for a moutain-fold line, score on the back. To make a neat fold line, cut at a depth of one-third of the thickness of paper on the right side. If you don't fold exactly, you may not obtain the desired shape. Begin folding from the corner of the longer fold lines using both hands. For the shorter fold lines, use the point of tweezers and fold exactly.

The base :

All the 90° open type cards are made of a sheet of paper with pop-up design. However, if you use another sheet of Kent paper of the same color or drawing paper in contrasting color for the base, an interesting effect can be added to the card. Paper of the same size as the card is often used for the base (20cm by 15cm (8″×6″) or 30cm by 10cm (12″×4″), etc.), but if you glue two sheets of 10cm by 15cm (4″×6″) paper separately onto each half of the card, you don't have to crease the center fold line and you can easily open the card. Use all-purpose glue for attaching the base. Carefully apply glue to the corners.

2. To make the 180° open type card :

It is sometimes difficult for a beginner to picture a completed three-dimensional design. However, I can say the 180° open type cards encompass all the most interesting features of pop-up designs. Please try making original cards following the instructions below.

Cut out parts :

The pattern for parts, unfolded shape and ground plan are shown for the 180° open type card. Cut the required number of parts as indicated.

Assemble the parts :

Assemble the parts following the photo. The points for assembling are given for each project, but think carefully before you start.

Attach cotton threads to the assembled parts :

The assembled parts are attached to the base at three or four places with cotton threads (6-7cm) (2⅜″-2¾″). Each thread is glued with a small piece of Japanese rice paper (see Pine decoration on page 30). The places for attaching thread are indicated in the patterns. After assembling the parts, place them on the base and make sure of the exact points of attaching thread. Then, glue each thread with a small piece of Japanese rice paper.

Insert threads into holes and fix :

Insert the ends of thread into the holes of the base, pull thread and fix onto the base temporarily with clear adhesive tape. Check whether the assembled parts pop up when the card is opened. If it works well, fix the end of each thread with glued Japanese rice paper. Trim off excess thread.

Attach another sheet of paper for backing :

Using another sheet of white Kent paper, back the base for reinforcement and for a neater finish. If you use two sheets of 15cm by 10cm (6″×4″) paper, the card can be opened easily. Glue a small piece of Kent paper onto each piece of Japanese rice paper as a final touch.

Montage B, shown on page 12.

Key to the lines :

————————— Cutting line

— — — — — Mountain fold line (convex)

·············· Valley fold line (concave)

Mountain-fold lines and valley-fold lines are shown in reverse in this pattern.
Use this side as the back of the card. The pattern pops up on the reverse side.

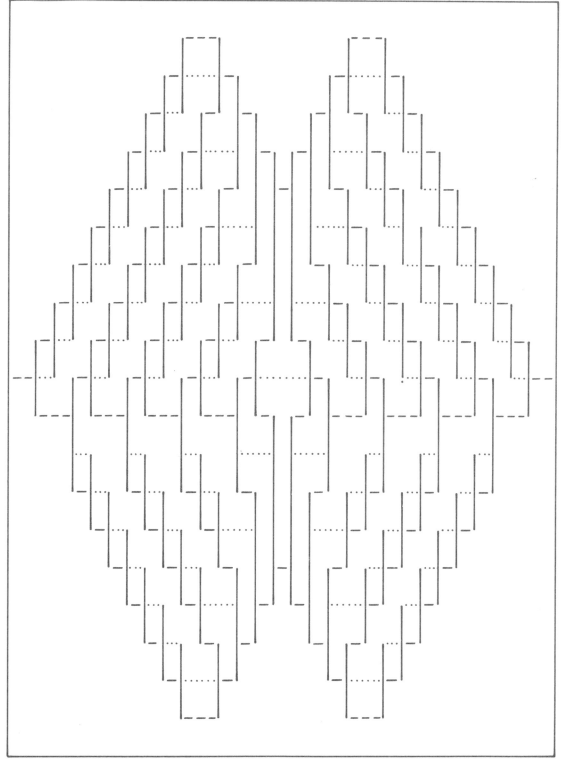

Stairs to Paradise D, *shown on page 15.*

Key to the lines :

———————— Cutting line

— — — — — Mountain fold line (convex)

·············· Valley fold line (concave)

Mountain-fold lines and valley-fold lines are shown in reverse in this pattern.
Use this side as the back of the card. The pattern pops up on the reverse side.

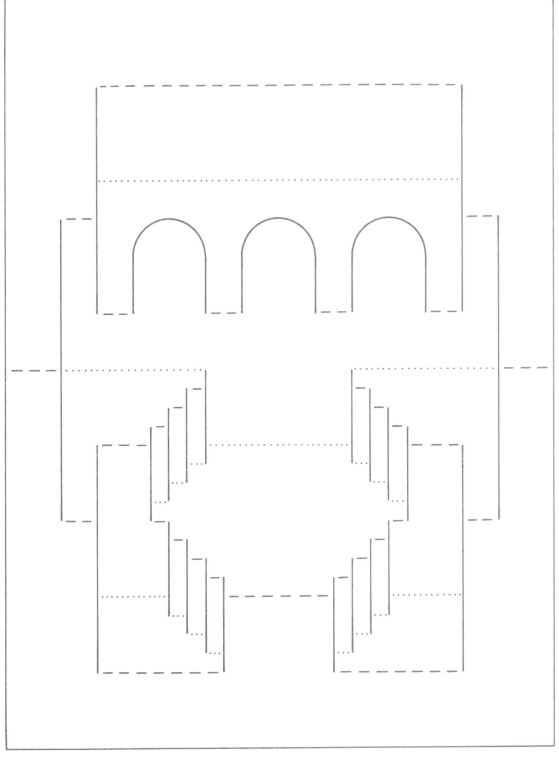

Dining Car, *shown on page 17.*

Key to the lines :

———————— Cutting line

– – – – – Mountain fold line (convex)

·············· Valley fold line (concave)

Mountain-fold lines and valley-fold lines are shown in reverse in this pattern.
Use this side as the back of the card. The pattern pops up on the reverse side.

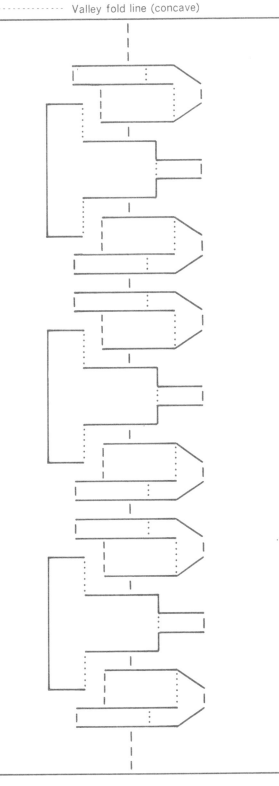
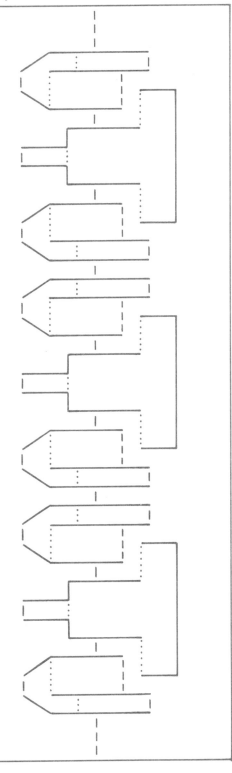

Circular Construction B, shown on page 20.

Key to the lines:

——————— Cutting line

— — — — — Mountain fold line (convex)

.... Valley fold line (concave)

Mountain-fold lines and valley-fold lines are shown in reverse in this pattern.
Use this side as the back of the card. The pattern pops up on the reverse side.

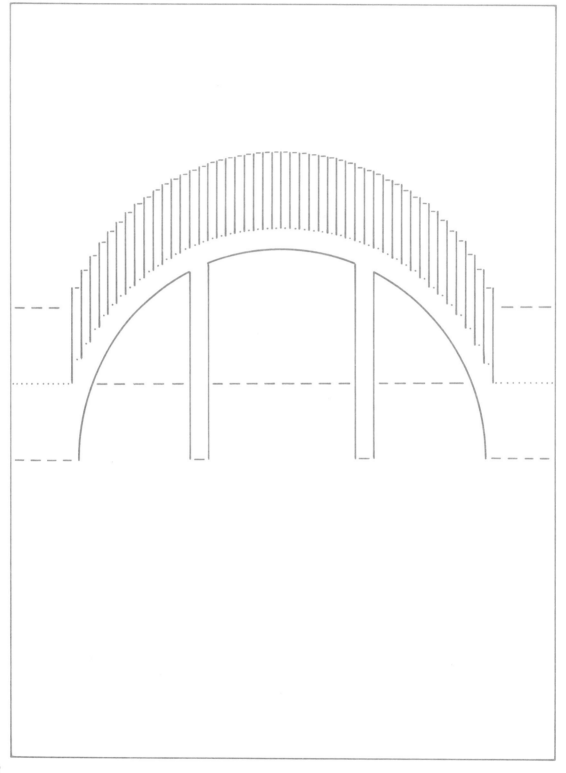